BION AND THOUGHTS TOO DEEP FOR WORDS

Distinguishing psychoanalysis, as a search for truth, from suggestion, as a cure for symptoms, this book addresses the scientific status of psychoanalysis. Citing research into the relationship of infants to their caretakers, the author discusses evidence that unconscious communication is present from birth, and that this form of communication plays a central role in psychoanalysis at a level below that of verbal communication.

Informed by Bion's ideas of containment, group functioning and the fundamental psychological need for truth, this book asserts that psychoanalysis, based solely on the search for truth, has, among all psychological interventions, both a unique claim to scientific status and a unique ability to foster psychological development.

Exploring the relationship between unconscious communication, group dynamics, containment and psychological development in a highly original way, *Bion and Thoughts Too Deep for Words: Psychoanalysis, Suggestion, and the Language of the Unconscious* will be of great interest to psychotherapists, psychologists and psychoanalysts who are interested in the relationship between psychoanalysis and suggestion.

Robert Caper, MD, is the author of three books and numerous articles on psychoanalysis. He has lectured in countries all around the world and currently resides in New York City and Vermont where he practices and teaches.

THE ROUTLEDGE WILFRED R. BION STUDIES BOOK SERIES
Howard B. Levine, MD
Series Editor

Editorial Advisory Board: Nicola Abel-Hirsch, Joseph Aguayo, Avner Bergstein, Lawrence J.Brown, Judith Eekhoff, Claudio Laks Eizerik, Robert D.Hinshelwood, Chris Mawson, James Ogilvie, Elias M. da Rocha Barros, Jani Santamaria, Rudi Vermote

The contributions of Wilfred Bion are among the most cited in the analytic literature. Their appeal lies not only in their content and explanatory value, but in their generative potential. Although Bion's training and many of his clinical instincts were deeply rooted in the classical tradition of Melanie Klein, his ideas have a potentially universal appeal. Rather than emphasizing a particular psychic content (e.g., Oedipal conflicts in need of resolution; splits that needed to be healed; preconceived transferences that must be allowed to form and flourish, etc.), he tried to help open and prepare the mind of the analyst (without memory, desire or theoretical preconception) for the encounter with the patient.

Bion's formulations of group mentality and the psychotic and non-psychotic portions of the mind, his theory of thinking and emphasis on facing and articulating the truth of one's existence so that one might truly learn first-hand from one's own experience, his description of psychic development (alpha function and container/contained) and his exploration of **O** are "non-denominational" concepts that defy relegation to a particular school or orientation of psychoanalysis. Consequently, his ideas have taken root in many places ... and those ideas continue to inform many different branches of psychoanalytic inquiry and interest.[1]

It is with this heritage and its promise for the future developments of psychoanalysis in mind that we present *The Routledge Wilfred R. Bion Studies Book Series*. This series gathers together under newly emerging and continually evolving contributions to psychoanalytic thinking that rest upon Bion's foundational texts and explore and extend the implications of his thought. For a full list of titles in the series, please visit the Routledge website at: www.routledge.com/The-Routledge-Wilfred-Bion-Studies-Book-Series/book-series/RWBSBS

Howard B. Levine, MD
Series Editor

---

1 Levine, H.B. and Civitarese, G. (2016). Editors' Preface, *The W.R. Bion Tradition*, Levine and Civitarese, eds., London: Karnac, 2016, p. xxi.

BION AND THOUGHTS TOO DEEP FOR WORDS

Psychoanalysis, Suggestion, and the Language of the Unconscious

Robert Caper

LONDON AND NEW YORK

First published 2020
by Routledge
2 Park Square, Milton Park, Abingdon, Oxon OX14 4RN

and by Routledge
52 Vanderbilt Avenue, New York, NY 10017

Routledge is an imprint of the Taylor & Francis Group, an informa business

© 2020 Robert Caper

The right of Robert Caper be identified as the author has been asserted in accordance with sections 77 and 78 of the Copyright, Designs and Patents Act 1988.

All rights reserved. No part of this book may be reprinted or reproduced or utilized in any form or by any electronic, mechanical, or other means, now known or hereafter invented, including photocopying and recording, or in any information storage or retrieval system, without permission in writing from the publishers.

Trademark notice: Product or corporate names may be trademarks or registered trademarks, and are used only for identification and explanation without intent to infringe.

British Library Cataloguing-in-Publication Data
A catalogue record for this book is available from the British Library

Library of Congress Cataloging-in-Publication Data
A catalog record has been requested for this book

ISBN: 978-0-367-44456-3 (hbk)
ISBN: 978-0-367-41845-8 (pbk)
ISBN: 978-1-003-00986-3 (ebk)

Typeset in Bembo
by Swales & Willis, Exeter, Devon, UK

CONTENTS

Preface *vi*

1 Song-and-dance 1
2 Song-and-dance and the internal world 8
3 The dynamics of unconscious communication 14
4 Psychoanalysis and suggestion 19
5 Psychoanalysis beyond suggestion 29
6 The analyst's Oedipal dilemma 34
7 Psychoanalysis and science 45
8 The craft of psychoanalysis 54
9 Psychoanalysis and play 68
10 Containment, self-containment and identification 74
11 Finding the context 87
12 Summary and conclusions 94

Index *100*

PREFACE

The unconscious, like the past, is another country. They do things differently there.

In the roughly twelve decades since psychoanalysis first emerged from its origins in hypnosis and suggestion with Freud's discovery of the dynamic unconscious, it has evolved into a powerful tool for freeing the mind through study of this previously unknown country.

In this book, I assess some of what psychoanalysis (along with the allied field of infant observation) has revealed about the ways of this unconscious country, including its language, which occupies a previously unrecognized register. Clinical psychoanalysis is the translation of the language of the unconscious into language accessible to consciousness. The barriers to this translation bring to mind the closing lines of William Wordsworth's "Intimations of Immortality":

> Thanks to the human heart by which we live,
> Thanks to its tenderness, its joys, and fears,
> To me the meanest flower that blows can give
> Thoughts that do often lie too deep for tears.

The deepest layers of the internal object world, lying somewhere on the border of mind and body, imbue the meanest flowers of the external world with the emotionality that gives them psychological significance. This internal world lies too deep for words. Its true language, as befits its bodily origins, is visceral, kinaesthetic and sonorous. Psychoanalysts, though lacking Wordsworth's gifts, nonetheless presume to make a clinical practice of translating it into ordinary words, muddling along as best we can.

—New York City and Worcester, Vermont, 2019

1
SONG-AND-DANCE

In 1966, William Condon, working at the University of Pittsburgh, devised a technique for observing conversations between adults using high-speed cinematography followed by a close, frame-by-frame analysis of the words and motions of the speaker and listener. Using this technique, Condon was able to detect body movements too ephemeral to be visible to the naked eye. These films revealed what he described in retrospect as "two sets of interesting and consistent findings" that he called self-synchrony and interactional synchrony. In the formal language of academic science, he wrote,

> "Self-synchrony" refers to the integrated behavior of the individual in which correspondence can be demonstrated, for example, between the film frame of occurrence of a change in sound elements of his own speech and the film frame of occurrence of a change in his own body movements. "Interactional synchrony" designates a similar correspondence between change in sound elements in the speech of a speaker and points of change in movement configurations shown by the listener. These synchronies are not readily detectable at normal communication speed, appear to occur primarily in relation to speech, and are usually totally out of awareness of the individuals so engaged.
>
> *(Condon and Sander, 1974, p. 456)*

In other words, speakers, without being aware of it, dance in subtle ways to the rhythms of their speech, and their listeners do the same. This duet of song-and-dance is deficient or absent in individuals with impaired capacity to communicate, such as those suffering from aphasia, autism or schizophrenia.[1]

What was most surprising about this work was the observation that infants as young as two days also danced in response to adult speech:

2 Song-and-dance

[One] 2-day-old neonate sustained equally synchronous segments of change of movement [that is, as synchronous as those of adult listeners] with the adult's speech across [a] full 89-word sequence. In other words, this is in no way accidental but a sustained and precise concurrence. Another 2-day-old sustained movement synchronous throughout, with a series of 125 words of female speech presented by tape recorder ... [This] precision of synchronization ... was found to characterize the correspondence between adult speech and infant movement in all 16 infants [studied]. Fourteen of these infants were from 12 hours to 2 days old and two others were at 14 days after birth. The correspondence occurred whether the adult speaker was actually present and talking to the neonate, or whether the voice came from a tape recorder. An audiotape containing American English, isolated vowel sounds, tapping sounds, and Chinese language excerpts was used as a stimulus, as well as a living adult speaker. Two of the infants were held, and the rest were supine in their cribs. Chinese, presented to American neonates, was associated with as clear a correspondence as was American English. Disconnected vowel sounds, however, failed to show the degree of correspondence which was associated with natural rhythmic speech. Tapping sounds also failed to show correspondence except at times when occurring in proximity to speech.

(Condon and Sander, 1974, p. 461)

These observations lead Condon to a perspective on human communication from which one sees infants pre-programmed to respond to the rhythms and tones of adult speech. He suggests an inquiry into human communication as "an expression of participation within shared organizational forms rather than isolated entities sending discrete messages." The responsivity of infants to human speech rhythms literally recruits them bodily into what Condon calls the "shared organization" of human vocal communication long before they are able to understand the semantic content of words.[2]

Infants seem to have the ability to distinguish meaningless voice sounds ("isolated vowel sounds") from meaningful speech. In other words, they are able to detect the presence of meaning in human speech long before they understand its semantic content. A significant portion of the meaning conveyed by speech must therefore be non-semantic. This may seem surprising until we recall the direct emotional impact of music. Human speech consists of strings of words that have meaning and syntax. Whatever their meaning, these words are normally uttered with rhythm, variations in loudness, and variations in pitch. These fundamental elements of human speech are equally fundamental elements of music.[3] What Condon discovered was that people dance to the music of speech—their own and others. This dance begins at least as early as the day of birth, when there is no question of the semantic content of speech having any impact. The music of speech "entrains" dance-like movement, and the infant is first recruited into the linguistic community by being given music it can dance to. Language is not simply something learned by children from adults. It is also a vehicle through which what Condon calls innate human organizational forms may be shared and joined.

Donald Meltzer has proposed that the genesis of language is

> essentially two-tiered, having a primitive song-and-dance level (the most primitive form of symbol-formation) for the communication of emotional states of mind ... and that upon this foundation of deep grammar there is subsequently superimposed the lexical level of words for denoting objects, actions and qualities of the external world, that is, information.
> *(Meltzer, 1986, p. 181)*

What we might ordinarily regard as language is only a part of language, and not its most fundamental part. Meltzer distinguishes between a deep musical language, used for communicating about the internal world (that is, states of mind), upon which is built a more superficial, lexical language useful for communicating about the external, material world.[4] Michael Paul (1989) has described the rhythm, pace and intonation of patients' speech, and how their difficulties in thinking about or understanding interpretations may be quite effectively addressed by focussing their attention on the elements of their speech that seem designed to interfere with understanding and contact with oneself. He describes the music of resistance.

Susan Maiello (2013) points out that the foetus has the capacity to hear from mid-gestation onward, and that this capacity is stimulated regularly by the sound of the mother's voice and heartbeat. Even after this experience is interrupted by birth, rhythmic sound and movements will calm the newborn.[5] She adds that awareness of the presence of the mother's voice also sets the stage for awareness of its absence, an important developmental achievement: "This voice being present could be the first source of comfort, but also it could give a sensation of absence or vacuum when it isn't heard, setting the following empty space in which ... thought will be born" (Maiello, 2013).

In a related observation, Ellen Dissanayake has observed that rhythmic movement in groups—dance—has the effect of entraining the minds of the participant individuals in a powerful and characteristic way. She observes that "simply keeping together in time with other persons produces a feeling of well-being or euphoria", and goes on to recall that,

> The historian, William H. McNeill (1995) has given a name—"muscular bonding"—to the phenomenon of fellow feeling that he experienced as a young army draftee during close-order drill, and speculates that it evolved because of its contribution to group solidarity. He described it as "a strange sense of personal enlargement; a sort of swelling out, becoming bigger than life".
> *(Malloch and Trevarthen, 2009, p. 539)*

Dissanayake's interpretation of this is that, "In ceremonies, bodies swayed to music result in minds relieved of existential anxieties, firmed by convictions, and bonded with their fellows in a common cause" (ibid., p. 542).

4 Song-and-dance

A third line of observation about the mutual unconscious responsiveness of humans to other humans is the so-called "still-face experiment" devised by Edward Tronick and his colleagues in 1975 and widely used as a research tool since that time. It concerns what appears to be an exquisite early sensitivity to physical mien (Tronick, 1989). A witness to one of Tronick's presentations of this work wrote,

> First, a split screen image of a 70-day-old infant and his mother appeared on the conference ballroom's big screen as they engaged in the pleasant cyclic ebb and flow of a face-to-face interaction. Then, the dyad reappeared in a "still-face" condition during which the mother remained "completely unresponsive, with a flat expressionless face for 3 minutes."
>
> The infant first orients toward the mother and greets her expectantly. But when the mother fails to respond appropriately, the infant "rapidly sobers and grows wary. He makes repeated attempts to get the interaction into its usual reciprocal pattern. When these attempts fail, the infant orients his face and body away from his mother with a withdrawn, hopeless facial expression." This is soon followed by tearful distress.
>
> *(Adamson and Frick, 2003, pp. 462–463)*

These observations indicate that infants respond not only to the music of human speech, but also to human facial expression, and that a responsive face has an organizing or animating effect on an infant, while an unresponsive face where a responsive one was anticipated can lead to withdrawal, despair and disorganization.

Condon showed that infants organize themselves physically in tune with the music of speech, while Tronick showed that they depend on a live, responsive face to maintain their psychological organization. McNeill's observations about "muscular bonding" suggest that rhythmic group movement—line dancing—produces a sense of enlargement that transcends the boundaries of the individual—another example of "shared organization".

Speech, body movement, and facial expression are the major conduits through which people convey emotion. Infants appear to be sensitive to these kinds of expression from birth onward, and are able to use it to obtain a direct read of the emotional states of other people. Furthermore, there appears to be a need in even very young infants to synchronize or align their emotional state with that of others, and to receive feedback that this has occurred, if they are to avoid psychological disorganization. It is hard to resist the idea that humans are born with a capacity to interpret subtle cues of facial expression and vocal intonation and rhythm. This capacity appears so soon after birth that it is hard to imagine it being learned so quickly simply from interactions with other humans.

In a recent review of the past forty years of research on the role of song-and-dance in human interaction, Stephen Malloch and Colwyn Trevarthen (2009), propose "a new theory of how human will and emotion are immediately shareable with others through gestures of the body and voice." They note that in this research, babies were found to be more aware of human presence and its activity and affections than they were of physical objects or events, and this strong curiosity for humans was expressed in responsive smiles, calls and gestures which excited their mothers and "captured" them into the flow of the present moment of the exchange.

(Malloch and Trevarthen, 2009, p. 1)

Note that the connection works both ways: the infant's smiles, calls and gestures exciting and captivating their mothers, recruiting them into a synchronous mental state with the infant, just as the mothers recruit them into their states by cooing, tonally exaggerated "baby talk" and singing. Music and dance are a two way street, creating a shared mental organization where there would otherwise be isolated individuals. So fundamental is the phenomenon of synchronization that we must question whether an "otherwise" of entirely discreet, disconnected individuals is ever really found.

This grouping is mediated not by the semantics of the words, but by the music of the voice and the dance of facial expression and physical gestures. Echoing Condon and Meltzer, Malloch and Trevarthen point out that this group connection is not communication in the ordinary sense of the word, since "the information carried by interpersonal rhythms does not move directly from one person to another. Thus information cannot easily be conceptualized as messages since the information is always simultaneously shared and always about the state of the relationship" (2009, p. 2).

This connection

> complements [verbal] language by providing us with a means for sharing coordinated, embodied space and time while lessening the potential for disagreements based on the particularity or "discretising" of verbal meaning... we can agree in the shared embodied space of music and dance, whereas we may disagree in the shared objective space of a verbal discussion because our version of "reality" differs from that of another.

They conclude that through this

> collaborative musicing,... our sense of separateness moves towards a sense of being an inseparable part of community... an experience [that may be called] "multi-subjective, in the sense that we both lose and retain our subjectivity within the collective" I... musicality's nature of engaging one with an other, or many with many, intersubjectively, is intrinsic to musicality's healing potential.

(2009, pp. 6–7)

Human animals draw each other automatically, regularly and irresistibly into each other's mental and emotional spheres, spontaneously forming communities marked by shared mental organization. This recruitment activity constitutes

6 Song-and-dance

a substantial part of everyday mental life. The universal, unconscious tendency for emotional synchronization produces a sense of enlargement or connection that transcends the boundaries of the individual, and gives rise to a rapport in which disagreements and discriminations that might occur on the basis of a verbal discussion are suppressed in favour of sharing a "coordinated, embodied space and time". This type of rapport is automatic, spontaneous, requires no thought, and is almost never completely resistible. It is, one might say, the natural default state of one human mind in contact with another.

The work I have just summarized draws our attention to the power of speech rhythms, along with bodily movement and facial expression, to affect the emotional state of others in a manner that is both direct and outside the awareness of either party. It appears that this unconscious song-and-dance connection is woven into the fabric of human relations, synchronizing people's emotional states. Language originates in this mental synchronization and only later becomes a lexical activity—a conscious activity of "isolated entities sending discreet messages" in which non-synchrony (individual discriminative thought) can be expressed. There is a powerful force, present near, at, or perhaps even before birth, that weaves humans together into a psychological commonality; discrete, non-communal psychological states arise only later, against the background of the earlier synchronized mental states. These discoveries expand our idea of language and communication beyond the verbal realm, and permit a perspective from which verbal communication, far from encompassing all of language, is only a later development that rests on an earlier musical foundation. This expansion of our concept of language echoes the expansion of our concept of mind brought about by the discovery of the unconscious, so that just as we now recognize that the conscious mind, previously thought to be the entire mind, is only its most superficial layer, we now also recognize that the conscious aspects of verbal language, previously regarded as the whole of it, are only *its* most superficial layer.

It is tempting to align these two discoveries by postulating that non-verbal modes of communication, operating outside of consciousness, form a direct link between the (non-verbal) unconscious of one mind and that of another, entering conscious life if at all only as a "vibe", a term that reveals its roots in the musical register. Restating this in slightly more rigorous psychoanalytic terms, this mode of communication may form a direct link between one person's unconscious internal world and that of another.

Notes

1 "Microanalyses of pathological behavior have revealed marked self-dyssynchronies, in which correspondence between linguistic elements and kinesic elements is reduced or absent: for example, these are encountered in subjects with aphasic, autistic, and schizophrenic conditions" (Condon and Sander, 1974, p. 458).
2 "The sustained synchrony of organized correspondences between adult speech and neonate body movement at this microkinesic level, within periods lasting less than a second, raises issues about the nature of communication across many levels. It would

suggest that infant motor organization, entrained by the organized pattern of adult speech over many months from birth, may be preparing operational formats emerging toward a later, and also developmental, implanting of speech. It thus suggests inquiry into the 'bond' between human beings as an expression of participation within shared organizational forms rather than isolated entities sending discrete messages" (Condon and Sander, 1974, p. 462).

3 Early versions of computer-generated voices produced words strung together in syntactically correct sentences, but they sounded like machines trying to talk. Only after programmers learned to incorporate musical elements into their artificial voices did they begin to resemble human speech.

4 See also (Meltzer, 1975, p. 193).

5 Recall Freud's observation that "there is much more continuity between intra-uterine life and earliest infancy than the impressive caesura of the act of birth would have us believe" (Freud, 1926, p. 138).

Bibliography

Lauren B. Adamson and Janet E. Frick. The still face: A history of a shared experimental paradigm. *Infancy*, 4(4):451–473, 2003.

William S. Condon and Louis W. Sander. Synchrony demonstrated between movements of the neonate and adult speech. *Child Development*, 45(2):456–462, 1974. ISSN 00093920, 14678624. URL www.jstor.org/stable/1127968.

Sigmund Freud. Inhibitions, symptoms and anxiety. *The Standard Edition of the Complete Psychological Works of Sigmund Freud*, 20:75–172, 1926.

Suzanne Maiello. On the origins of language: Vocal and rhythmic aspects of the primary relationship and its absence in autistic states. *Controversy in Children and Adolescent Psychoanalysis*, 13:23–51, 2013. URL http://controversiasonline.org.ar/PDF/anio2013-n13-en/5.MAIELLO-ING.pdf.

Stephen Malloch and Colwyn Trevarthen. *Communicative Musicality: Exploring the Basis of Human Companionship*. Oxford University Press, Oxford, UK, 2009.

William Hardy McNeill. *Keeping Together in Time: Dance and Drill in Human History*. Harvard University Press, Massachusetts, USA, 1995.

Donald Meltzer. *Explorations in Autism*. Clunie Press, Perthshire, UK, 1975.

Donald Meltzer. *Studies in Extended Metapsychology: Clinical Application of Bion's Ideas*. Clunie Press, Perthshire, UK, 1986.

M. I. Paul. Intonational elements as communication in psychoanalysis. *Free Associations*, 1:67–86, 1989.

E. Z. Tronick. Emotions and emotional communication in infants. *The American Psychologist*, 44:112–119, February 1989. ISSN 0003-066X.

2
SONG-AND-DANCE AND THE INTERNAL WORLD

Projective identification

In 1946, the British psychoanalyst Melanie Klein described a phenomenon she had observed in her work with small children, consisting of unconscious fantasies of expelling parts of their minds into other people, and of incorporating parts of other people's minds into their own. This "balance of projection and introjection" (or "projective identification", as she later called it) is a mental function that would produce precisely the kind of non-discreteness of minds and automatic, preverbal mental synchronization that Condon, Tronick and Trevarthen have hypothesized on the basis of their observations of infant behaviour.

In 1962, one of Klein's students, Wilfred Bion, refined this idea when he proposed the existence of what he called "realistic projective identification". Using the theoretical language of infant and mother to stand for patient and analyst, he wrote:

> Ordinarily the personality of the infant, like other elements in the environment, is managed by the mother. If the mother and child are adjusted to each other, projective identification plays a major role in the management; the infant is able through the operation of a rudimentary reality sense to behave in such a way that projective identification, usually an omnipotent phantasy, is a realistic phenomenon. This, I am inclined to believe, is its normal condition ... As a realistic activity it shows itself as behaviour reasonably calculated to arouse in the mother feelings of which the infant wishes to be rid.
>
> *(Bion, 1967, p. 308)*

In an Afterword to their comprehensive review of projective identification, Spillius and O'Shaughnessey suggested expanding the scope of the term projective identification beyond infancy and psychoanalysis:

In our view, the concept of projective identification is not particular to the clinical situation but a universal of human communication, one that Freud was questing for. In 1915 in his paper "The Unconscious", he writes: "It is a very remarkable thing that the Ucs. [unconscious] of one human being can react upon that of another, without passing through the Cs. [conscious]. This deserves closer investigation" (Freud, 1915, p. 194). And later, in 1933, he again describes this process. "There is, for example, the phenomenon of thought-transference … It claims that mental processes in one person—ideas, emotional states, conative impulses—can be transferred to another person through empty space without employing the familiar methods of communication by means of words and signs" (Freud, 1933, p. 39).

We think that the concept of projective identification gives a name to, and a clarification of, the dynamics of direct communication and the phenomena of transference and countertransference that are universal among humankind.

(Spillius and O'Shaughnessey, 2012)

Bion's observation about the human capacity to evoke emotional states in another person without either party being aware of the evocation points to the operation of something very much like the unconscious, non-lexical communication discussed in the previous chapter. The concept of projective identification gives us a psychoanalytic model of the dynamics of primitive song-and-dance. Music is not just the food of love, but, together with dance, the stuff of deep emotional communication, generating emotions that are themselves so deep that they are difficult to distinguish from bodily sensations.

The early development of the mind

Infants dance to the music of human speech. This implies that from birth onward they are receptive to the music of human speech (but not to randomly assembled speech sounds) and are capable of expressing its rhythms through bodily movement (a response absent if the stimulus is rhythmic mechanical sound). Song-and-dance is innate, requires some interaction or activity with someone outside the self, and seems to be necessary for the maintenance of the infant's psychological integrity, just as physical sustenance is necessary to the infant's physical survival.[1]

Bion assumed that we are born herd animals and that in the most primitive levels of our mentality we are overwhelmingly concerned with membership in our group (Meltzer, 1978, Part III, p. 9). That membership is a function of what he called the "proto-mental" part of the personality, a level of the mind in which physical events (sensations) are not differentiated from psychological events (emotions) (Bion, 1961). Arising at the same time as the infant's recruitment into the external human community is the establishment within the infant of an internal world that is partly a reflection of the external human community.

The relationship between this internal world and the external community is complex: it is an internal version of the external community with which it interacts via song-and-dance. The infant's internal object world is both a product of its interaction with the external human world and a requirement for this interaction. A live internal object world is the infant's ticket of admission to the mental and emotional community of other minds, a community that is formed by the connection of one internal world to another. The medium of this connection is one's musical recruitment of other minds into one's own and one's musical absorption by and into other minds. From the infant's point of view, the external community of minds expresses and mirrors the internal world of emotional psychic reality, and the internal world incorporates other minds as they are made available through song-and-dance. There is room in our minds for other minds. Taking into account the emotional and feeling level on which these events transpire, it would perhaps be better to say that there is room in our hearts for other hearts.

Melanie Klein's theories of projective identification and of the internal world describe mental operations that support these mind-to-mind connections. These operations take place in the register of concrete unconscious fantasies. Musical (song-and-dance) communication is not symbolic. Though it may subsequently be symbolized, it does not itself refer to anything other than itself: it simply evokes concrete experiences and is the natural mode of communication between one unconscious mind and another.

Song-and-dance communication is one source contributing to the formation of Klein's internal world. The other is sensations and urges generated by somatic processes—i.e., instincts. The internal world is experienced first as activity within the body, an experience that persists throughout life in the deeper levels of the unconscious. In Klein's view, the internal world is inhabited by what she called "internal objects", a term that,

> exactly expresses what the child's unconscious, and for that matter the adult's in deep layers, feels about it. In these layers it is not felt to be part of the mind in the sense, as we have learnt to understand it, of the super-ego being the parents' voices inside one's mind. This is the concept we find in the higher strata of the unconscious. In the deeper layers, however, it is felt to be a physical being, or rather a multitude of beings, which with all their activities, friendly and hostile, lodge inside one's body, particularly inside the abdomen, a conception to which physiological processes and sensations of all kinds, in the past and in the present, have contributed.[2]

Intuition and the internal world

The vehicle of direct communication between peoples' unconscious internal worlds is the non-semantic (song-and-dance) aspects of language. While we communicate about the physical world using conscious symbolic thought and the semantic aspects of language, communication between unconscious internal worlds takes place on the register of song-and-dance.

The power of music and dance to both express and elicit visceral emotion—emotion felt in the body—is a part of everyone's experience; the dance response of infants to the music of speech suggests that we tune in from birth to song-and-dance directly with our bodies. Bodily experiences are the earliest and, throughout life, most fundamental locus of Klein's unconscious internal world.

While we can detect the inanimate physical world, and the behaviour of others, with our sensory apparatus, awareness of another person's internal state requires the apparatus of intuition.[3] Intuition is, therefore, a kind of music appreciation, tuned in to the major mode of unconscious communication, the register of song-and-dance.

The logically rigorous symbolic language of science is adequate for the description of the world of external (physical) phenomena, but so far has not proven adequate for the description of the phenomenology of the unconscious mind. For that, one seems to need the older language of bodily and musical expression, with its psychological and emotional vitality and paradoxical coexistence of opposites. The psychoanalyst's task is to express the music of unconscious phenomena using the lexical language of the conscious mind. How to do this, short of becoming a poet, is a challenging question. Over a long period, however, psychoanalyst and patient do seem to develop a language that is known to both and is more or less up to the task. Perhaps the slow development of this private language is one reason an analysis takes as long as it does and cannot be hurried.

Song-and-dance and the internal world

Song-and-dance communicates animate, unconscious internal realities directly from one person to another. These realities are intuited rather than being processed symbolically; their significance is felt in the body rather than being decoded by the intellect (that is, their effect, like that of music, is immediate, emotional, and non-verbal). The impact of song-and-dance on the minds of those involved bypasses critical discrimination and reasoning; it has an immediate effect on one's unconscious internal world and consequently one's conscious state of mind. This earliest form of communication between people starts at birth and is vital for mental development.

The deep levels of unconscious internal world, located on the border between bodily sensation and mental experience, are the source of emotionality. The origins of emotionality in bodily sensation are evident in the language we use to describe emotional states. "My heart sank", "that made me ill", "I've got the weight of the world on my shoulders", "that really burned me", "my heart's in my throat", "his heart leapt for joy", "she gives me a headache", "heart-warming", "I've had a belly full", "I have a gut feeling", and so on.

12 Song-and-dance and the internal world

The music and dance of Condon's "shared organization" conveys emotional experience directly and unconsciously. Observations of infants strongly indicate that this kind of communication plays a vital role of the development of the infant's and young child's mind. If conscious communication means exchanging discreet and deliberate messages with one another, unconscious communication means seeping insensibly, involuntarily and unwittingly into each other's minds.

It is likely that the internal world is formed by something like this insensible mutual seeping between the mind of the infant and the minds of those it is in contact with. Two elements seem to be needed for the infant's internal world to develop. The first is the state of mind of the external person with whom the infant is in contact, for example, a mother's love for the infant, conveyed through the song-and-dance, non-semantic communication between mother and infant. The second is the infant's capacity to recognize this love—his possession of a "receptor" in his internal world that enables him to intuit it, so to speak. This receptor turns out to be the infant's own love for its mother. Both of these elements are communicated by song-and-dance.

The importance for psychological development of the infant's having a well-functioning receptor for its mother's love may be seen by considering the consequences of failing to develop one. In his book *Learning from Experience* (1962), Bion describes a patient whose thought processes lacked the qualities of depth, resonance, and evocativeness that one associates with the human mind, and so seemed to be the product not of a mind, but of a machine. From the data of the patient's analysis, he draws a picture of the mental "organ" whose impairment resulted in this state of affairs, and reconstructs how it might have gotten that way. This reconstruction is worth recounting in some detail.

He begins by taking seriously the commonplace that, just as infants need physical care and comfort, they must also receive love. From this it follows that an infant must have the capacity to perceive love—a "sense organ" for love—much as it has sense organs for perceiving food and warmth.

He considers what might happen if something interfered with the infant's ability to take in those of its mother's states of mind that constitute its emotional sustenance. This could occur if, for example, the infant were unable to bear the emotional strain of realizing that its well-being—and even its survival—depended on something as intangible as its mother's love. In its horror of needing what is intangible, and therefore not possessable, the infant blinds itself to these needs and to the love, solace and understanding that would remind it of them. Starved of the requirements for mental and emotional growth, but unable to grasp them, it redoubles its desperate efforts to obtain what it can still perceive: material satisfactions divorced from emotional gratification.

In consequence, the infant grows into an adult like Bion's patient, who greedily pursued every form of material comfort in a vain effort to supply himself with the non-material comfort he lacked but could not recognize. He eventually comes to live in a perceptual world composed only of material objects, and inevitably becomes like a material object himself, a state of affairs reflected in his machine-like thought processes. To Bion, this represents a "breakdown in the patient's equipment for thinking" about emotional realities, which leaves him living in a universe populated by emotionless objects that Bion calls inanimate: "the breakdown in animism affects the capacity of the individual to transform sense impressions into material suitable for use in dream-thoughts [that is, thinking]" (Bion, 1992, pp. 133–134). In Bion's view, creation of such unpersonified, meaningless, psychologically dead internal objects destroys the ability to think in other than a machine-like way.

A person incapable of recognizing (intuiting) the emotional valence of interpersonal events (that is, incapable of operating in the register of song-and-dance) is a person unable to think like a person.

Notes

1 Observations such as Schlossman's (1926) about hospitalism in infants suggest that song-and-dance interactions are essential to life. If the required interaction fails, the infant falls apart and, in many cases, dies. Physical sustenance can, at least in principle, be delivered mechanically, but the satisfaction of emotional needs is delivered through the music and dance of speech, holding, rocking, soothing, caressing, cooing, and so on. It cannot be provided by a machine, because a machine cannot establish emotional contact with an infant.
2 D16, Melanie Klein Trust papers, Wellcome Library; quoted in Hinshelwood (1997, p. 885).
3 The importance of intuitive knowledge of other people's minds can be seen from the deficit of intuition present in clinical autism. Those suffering from it must simulate emotional contact by deducing qualities such as friendliness and hostility from behavior because they cannot intuit them directly. The disability associated with autistic states highlights the importance of direct emotional intuition.

Bibliography

Wilfred Bion. *Experiences in Groups*. Basic Books, New York, 1961.
Wilfred Bion. *Learning from Experience*. Heinemann, London, 1962. (also in: *Seven Servants*, Jason Aronson, New York, 1977).
Wilfred Bion. A theory of thinking. In *Second Thoughts*, 110–119. William Heinemann, London, 1967. Originally published in the *International Journal of Psycho-Analysis*, 43, 1962.
Wilfred Bion. *Cogitations*. Karnac, London, 1992.
Sigmund Freud. The unconscious. *The Standard Edition of the Complete Psychological Works of Sigmund Freud*, 14, 1915.
Sigmund Freud. New introductory lectures on psycho-analysis. *The Standard Edition of the Complete Psychological Works of Sigmund Freud*, 22:64–145, 1933.
R. D. Hinshelwood. The elusive concept of "internal objects": Its role in the formation of the Klein group. *The International Journal of Psycho-Analysis*, 78(5): 877–897, 1997.
Donald Meltzer. *The Kleinian Development*. Clunie Press, Perthshire, UK, 1978.
F. E. Schlossman. *Frage des hospitalismus im sauglingsaustalten*. Zeitschrift fur Kinderheilkunde, Berlin, 1926.
Elizabeth Spillius and Edna O'Shaughnessey. *Projective Identification: The Fate of a Concept*. Routledge, Abingdon, 2012.

3
THE DYNAMICS OF UNCONSCIOUS COMMUNICATION

Basic assumption activity

In his book *Experiences in Groups* (1961), Bion described an experiment that he conducted in the late 1940s under the auspices of the Tavistock Institute in London, in which he convened groups of people whose sole purpose was to study the group's own behaviour. Among his findings was the consistent presence in the groups of what he called a "group mentality", which could perhaps best be described as an unconscious idea, fantasy or belief of great emotional import held in common by the members of the group that provides them with both an emotional *raison d'être*—a passion—for group life and a sense of security about their ability to solve the problems they face as a group. He called this idea the group's "basic assumption", and the mentality that it represented "basic assumption mentality". In this mode of group mental functioning, the predominant link between the members is an automatic and unspoken sharing of the basic assumption idea, which acts as a kind of glue linking the minds of the individuals in the group. To denote the group members' potential for uniting in a basic assumption mentality, Bion suggested the term "valency".

In chemistry, valency is the capacity of one atom to combine with another. Bion borrowed this term "to express a capacity for instantaneous involuntary combination of one individual with another for sharing and acting on a basic assumption" (1961, p. 153). He wrote that,

> although I use [valency] to describe phenomena that are visible as, or deducible from, psychological events, yet I wish also to use it to indicate a readiness to combine on levels that can hardly be called mental at all but are characterized by behaviour in the human being that is more analogous to tropism[1] in plants than to purposive behaviour such as is implicit in a word like "assumption".
>
> *(1961, pp. 116–117)*

Like Bion's group valency, the inborn human capacity to enter into what Condon called "shared organizational forms" and into what Malloch and Trevarthen called the "shared embodied space of music and dance", is a tropism. It is an unconscious, spontaneous, and, among psychologically intact individuals, universal receptivity to psychological synchronization between the individuals in a group, who, were it to disappear, would feel a paralyzing sense of isolation (recall Tronick's still-face experiment). The musically based sharing of mental space actually alters one's sense of reality so that it aligns with that of other communicants. What valency does not allow is what Malloch and Trevarthen called "discretizing" (deviating from synchronized mental activity through the use of critical thought). The basic assumption of the basic assumption mode is a belief that is shared via synchronization by all members of a group, not because they are aware of evidence for it, but because such shared belief is driven by the emotional power of the group's "shared organizational forms" and the fact that sharing it produces a secure sense of belonging.

As examples of basic assumption groups, Bion, following Freud's work on groups (1921) gave the Church and the Army. The basic assumption idea of the Church is that there is a benign and omnipotent deity that loves and will care for the members of the Church. The basic assumption idea in the Army is that violence, sufficient in amount and timing, will solve the problems facing the group.

Bion held that the "leader" of the basic assumption group—the one whose lead everyone in the group follows—is not a person, but the basic assumption idea. An individual may become the de facto leader of the group only to the degree that he embodies the basic assumption idea, which is shared in a silent but pervasive way by all members of the group. The fact of this synchronized sharing is communicated among the group members in ways that, although quite powerful, are so subtle as to escape notice. Any member of the group not endorsing the shared idea will find that, to the extent that he manifests this disbelief, his existence will cease to be acknowledged by the group. He will find himself in the position of the baby in Tronick's still-face experiment. Likewise, a nominal group leader who fails to embody the shared idea fully is immediately replaced by someone who will. He must show himself to be a passionate believer in the active basic assumption if his powers as a leader are not to wither.[2]

In the shared emotional organization of the basic assumption mode, there is no room for critical thought that would lead to the possibility of one deviating from the predominant basic assumption of the group. The activity of the basic assumption group,

> judged by ordinary standards of social intercourse ... is almost devoid of intellectual content. Furthermore, if we note how assumptions [in the basic assumption group] pass unchallenged as statements of fact, and are accepted as such, it seems clear that critical judgement is almost entirely absent.
>
> *(Bion, 1961, p. 39)*

Members of the group feel that belief in the operative basic assumption is vital to the survival of the group as a source of security, and they regard critical questioning of the basic assumption as an undermining of the bond that holds the group together and a threat to the continued existence of the group. Adherence to these beliefs is accompanied by a deep feeling is that critical thought about them (such as an open-minded examination of atheistic ideas in a church or pacifistic ones in a military organization) is both immoral and a threat to the group's survival. Like the song-and-dance activity that it so closely resembles in its communalism, basic-assumption activity is both innate and fundamental. Critical examination of the operative basic assumption belief is a serious and difficult matter because it requires one to step outside the default synchronized mode of human bonding and communication. The group operating in the basic-assumption mode reacts with anxiety and hostility to scepticism about the utility or reality of its basic assumptions, precisely because scepticism threatens the bond that holds the group together and the possibility of communion based on that bond.

Work activity

Basic assumption activity is one of the two major modes of group mental functioning in Bion's account of his experiences in groups. The other is what he called "work group activity". In work group activity, the group is preoccupied not with a dogma, or a leader embodying a dogma, but with the pragmatic reality of the problems at hand. The work group values connection to reality as measured by practical results—progress towards the group's realistic goals—regardless of the level of anxiety generated by this activity.

In the work mode, the group is in a position to observe the realities and problems that confront it in a realistic way. Among these realities are the limits imposed on the group by the fact that its understanding of the problems that face it is limited; that it has a finite time in which to solve these problems; that, even if it understood these problems perfectly, its power to effect solutions to them is circumscribed; and that experimentation both absorbs precious time and is hazardous. Awareness of these facts combine to produce a sense of insecurity that the group must tolerate if it is to perform its work, since work requires above all engagement with the realities of the problems on which it is working. In contrast to the sense of security associated with basic-assumption activity, work-group activity is characterized by a sense of insecurity and uncertainty.

Both work activity and basic assumption activity are present together in the group as different aspects of its functioning. A pure basic assumption group would be completely unable to face reality and would sooner or later experience an unexpected and disastrous collision with it. The members of a pure work group—a group completely unable to indulge in comforting delusions about its power—will sooner or later be overwhelmed by a sense of isolation, weakness and anxiety. A well-functioning group must somehow find a way to harbour both work group activity and basic assumption activity within itself, without either one destroying the other. This antinomy produces a tension that is characteristic of a well-functioning group.

Psychoanalysis as a group activity

Bion's observations were specifically about his "Tavistock" groups, whose task was to study their own functioning and that had no agenda other than this reflective activity. This is, of course, the same task as that of psychoanalysis, which makes Bion's observations about groups especially relevant to our understanding of psychoanalysis. We may consider the patient/analyst dyad in psychoanalysis as a Bionian group of two: two people meeting together for the purpose of studying what happens between them. No work group (i.e. no psychoanalysis) can evade basic assumption activity (although it may delude itself that it has), so all psychoanalyses must somehow cope with it if any work is to be done. If psychoanalysis is a group of two whose work it is to study itself, one way of characterizing its work would be to say that its purpose is to study, in a thoughtful way, the basic assumption activity that comes into play as a response to the anxieties and insecurities of the psychoanalytic work itself. Doing psychoanalysis produces insecurities in both patient and analyst that bring into play basic assumption activity, in the form of transference and countertransference, the study of which is the work of the analysis.

By studying and bringing to light the basic assumption activity in which it engages (and thereby both releasing and exposing to scrutiny the underlying anxieties against which the basic assumption activity protects the group of two), psychoanalysis creates the possibility of dealing with these anxieties without being trapped in basic assumption delusions, thus strengthening the work group and bringing about growth in its capacity to do psychoanalytic work—that is, its capacity to observe the forces shaping the relationship. All groups perform work, but the work of the psychoanalytic dyad is specifically to observe the emotional field in which it operates and thus to increase its capacity to observe the forces shaping the psychoanalytic relationship. The most powerful and pervasive of these forces are those carried on the pre-verbal register of song-and-dance.

Transference, countertransference, and basic assumption activity

Freud took transference to be the repetition of repressed past events within the current context of the analytic relationship. Today, many psychoanalysts recognize that transference is not a movement from past to present, but from inside to outside: what is transferred in transference is not the patient's repressed memories of past experiences with external objects, but the patient's current internal object world, and where it is transferred to is the external world of the analytic relationship. Transference is the name we give to the process whereby the analyst comes to represent not the patient's past external objects, but his current internal objects. It is a living biopsy of the patient's internal world.

To say that the analyst comes to represent for the patient his current internal objects in the transference is true as far as it goes, but it doesn't go farther than the most superficial layer of transference. On a deeper level, the patient may evoke in the analyst through the use of unconscious, song-and-dance projective identification emotional states that are congruent with his or her role in the patient's transference (Bion's "realistic projective identification"). The patient projects his internal objects into the analyst, where they take up residence in the analyst's internal world.

At the same time, the analyst's countertransference acts to shape the patient's internal world by driving the analyst to project his internal objects into the patient's inner world, also at the level of song-and-dance. If the transference and the countertransference are resonant, transference and countertransference act together to form a basic assumption idea producing a certain kind of basic assumption group.

An example of such a basic assumption group is one in which the patient, in his transference, needs the analyst to be an omnipotent healer (that is, has projected into the analyst an all-powerful healing object—a kind of god—from his inner world), and the analyst in his countertransference needs to be such a healer (that is, has projected into the patient an internal object in need of healing, and for which healing he feels responsible).

This type of basic assumption group is the basis of suggestion. The patient is vulnerable to suggestion from the analyst because he accepts the analyst's ideas uncritically in the desperate belief that doing so will cure him of his maladies. The analyst is vulnerable to making suggestions because of his need to cure himself of the problems associated with his internal objects by curing them in his patients.

Psychoanalysis brings a critical and discriminating focus to the deep emotionality involved in the uncritical, non-discriminating, and vital basic assumption relationships permeating the analysis. Psychoanalysis itself has had a long and complex relationship to the specific type of basic assumption activity known as suggestion. We shall examine this in detail in the next two chapters.

Notes

1 Tropism is the tendency of plants to grow in certain ways—for example, towards light (phototropism) or up from the ground (negative geotropism). The tropisms Bion decoded from the behavior of his groups correspond to what he called the "protomental" level of mental life.
2 As we shall see, these circumstances are the basis for the power of suggestion. If we picture the practitioner of suggestion as the leader of a group consisting of himself and his patient, both have a powerful motive to avoid scepticism. The patient believes because scepticism threatens to cut him off from the suggestionist's authority—a source of meaning and vitality—and the suggestionist believes because any hint of scepticism will diminish his power.

Bibliography

Wilfred Bion. *Experiences in Groups*. Basic Books, New York, 1961.
Sigmund Freud. Group psychology and the analysis of the ego. *The Standard Edition of the Complete Psychological Works of Sigmund Freud*, 18:69–143, 1921.

4
PSYCHOANALYSIS AND SUGGESTION

An example of a basic assumption belief in psychoanalysis is the tacit agreement between analyst and patient that the former knows the "healthy" direction in which the latter needs to go, and will shepherd him in that direction. Another is the tacit agreement that the so-called "good analytic relationship"—the analyst's patience, benignity and love will, over time, heal the patient. These basic assumptions must remain immune to critical thought if they are to retain their superordinate power. Certain questions must therefore not be raised in the basic assumption mode; for example, questions about evidence for the supposed wisdom of the analyst (or the supposed helplessness of the patient) in determining what is "healthy" for the patient, or questions about the idea that patience, tolerance, benevolence and love per se have healing powers.[1]

The shared organization of the group of two characterized by these basic assumptions underlies what has traditionally been called the power of suggestion. Psychoanalysis originated in the practice of suggestion, and the development of psychoanalysis over the more than 100 years of its existence is the history of its uncertain movement away from that practice. Freud began his career as a psychotherapist practising suggestion and hypnosis. At the time, suggestion consisted of little more than a crude attempt to force an idea into the patient's mind using the power of the suggestionist's dominant personality. Freud was not comfortable with this practice, as he indicated years later when he recalled witnessing the hypnotist Bernheim:

> I remember even then feeling a muffled hostility to this tyranny of suggestion. When a patient who showed himself unamenable was met with the shout: "what are you doing? Vous vous contre-suggestionnez!", I said to myself this was an evident injustice and an act of violence. For the man certainly had a right to counter-suggestions if people were trying to subdue him with suggestions.

(Freud, 1921, p. 89)

Freud found a potential solution to his misgivings when he heard from his older colleague Josef Breuer about a young female patient beset with dramatic hysterical symptoms, whom Breuer would visit daily for sessions of what the patient Bertha Pappenheim called chimney sweeping. Bertha would recount for Breuer the events of the day, with special emphasis on those that had upset her. Breuer would listen patiently, following which Bertha would experience a definite, although temporary, relief of her symptoms. They would repeat the procedure the following day, with similar results. Interruptions of the treatment would lead to deterioration of Bertha's condition, and its resumption to improvement.

Freud was impressed enough by Breuer's experience with Bertha to persuade him to collaborate on a book, *Studies in Hysteria* (Breuer and Freud, 1895), that chronicled Breuer's treatment of her, along with a number of cases of hysteria that Freud treated using Breuer's method (after having replaced the name "chimney sweeping" with "cathartic treatment"). Freud concluded the book with a theoretical exposition about the causes and treatment of hysteria—his so-called seduction theory of hysteria. This exposition followed the lines of an armchair theory of the brain and mind that he had been developing at the time, called "Psychology for Neurologists" (Freud, 1895). The availability of an explanation for the improvement that Breuer had seen in Bertha's condition that could be formulated in terms of what today would be called neuroscience no doubt encouraged the scientifically minded Freud to believe that the results were more profound and valid than those obtained by direct suggestion *à la* Bernheim.

Freud's theory postulated that the cause of hysteria was the sexual molestation of the patient when she (or he—Freud later reported cases of hysteria in male patients) was a child. This caused the child to become sexually excited. But, Freud argued, because the child's mental apparatus was immature, the excitation could not be discharged normally, as it would be in an adult (that is, by orgasm), and remained in the child's nervous system as an unmanageable (and hence damaging) stimulus, which is the definition of a trauma. The effect of this trauma was to damage the part of the nervous system concerned with receiving and discharging sexual excitation, the way an overload of current would damage part of an electrical circuit. The patient, now grown, could not remember the trauma because of the damage to the mental apparatus, and was left unable to react to sexual excitement in a normal way, thanks to the same damage. As a result, sexual excitation was diverted along abnormal neurological discharge pathways. The symptoms of hysteria were manifestations of this diversion.

Freud's theory of the mental/nervous apparatus implied that inducing the patient to recall in vivid emotional detail the traumatic experience of childhood would lance the psychological boil and allow the neurological burnout or blockade to heal. Whereas Breuer seemed to have been a passive and sympathetic listener to Bertha, Freud, under the influence of his theory of hysteria, began to delve deeper into the events surrounding his patient's symptomatic episodes, and to actively exert what he called "pressure" on the patient to overcome her repressions and to recall the original sexual trauma that had, as he thought, produced her illness. Freud's pressure technique was apparently quite forceful (at one point he actually exerted physical pressure on the patient's forehead to induce her to remember), and it is clear at least in retrospect that if this new form of suggestion was less crude and aggressive than Bernheim's, it was not by much.

Freud seems to have justified his own use of suggestion by distinguishing its aim from Bernheim's. While Bernheim aimed at simply getting the patient to get over a symptom by whatever means necessary, Freud, believed that the "pressure" approach attacked the patient's illness at its roots by getting to what he regarded as the truth of the patient's history, as stipulated in his theories of seduction and of psychological catharsis. He felt he was using the force of suggestion not to provide mere symptomatic relief, but to extirpate the cause of the illness.

Freud's theory about hysteria turned out to be almost entirely fanciful, as Krafft-Ebing, the president of the Vienna Medical Society none too gently pointed out to him, calling it a "scientific fairy tale" when Freud claimed success in seventeen cases of his cathartic treatment. He eventually abandoned the seduction theory in September 1897, not under the impact of Krafft-Ebing's criticism (which he resented), but because, contrary to what he had first claimed, and what his theory predicted, his successes in curing hysteria were only temporary.[2] The collapse of this theory in no way changed the fact that he had managed to obtain some real improvement, however temporary, in the symptoms of hysteria in a significant number of cases. But his successes did not rest on the validity of his theory; on the contrary, the theory was devised ad-hoc to account for the therapeutic success of his use of suggestion (his "cathartic method") with hysterical patients.[3]

Within a few months of abandoning his trauma/seduction theory, Freud devised a new one, very much like the old one but with one crucial difference: instead of assuming that repressed memories of sexual trauma were the source of the trouble, he assigned that role to repressed sexual fantasies and impulses. His therapeutic technique hardly changed with the new theory: instead of putting pressure on his patients to remember the repressed memory of sexual molestation, he pressured them to recognize the repressed sexual impulses which, he now felt, had led to the patient's illness. But with this relatively minor alteration, it was the same cathartic method, at whose heart lay the power of suggestion.[4]

As things stood at this point, hysteria was due to the repression of forbidden sexual wishes and impulses. These wishes did not cease to exist when repressed, but were merely relocated to a part of the mind separate from what one was aware of—the unconscious. Repression manifested itself clinically in two ways: as hysterical symptoms and as resistance to awareness of the repressed idea. Freud believed that the amount of pressure he needed to exert on the patient to get her to recall the repressed memory was a rough measure of the amount of resistance and repression keeping the wish unconscious.[5]

Over the next few years, from roughly 1897 to 1900, Freud gradually realized that it was not necessary to pressure his patients to express their repressed impulses in words. What his patients could not remember they acted out in their relationship with their analyst. What had supposedly been buried was in fact present at every moment in the analytic consulting room, enacted in full and exact detail, however thoroughly disguised. Freud called this aspect of the patient's relationship with him the transference. The transference is an illustration of Faulkner's dictum about the past.[6]

It is impossible to overestimate the importance of the discovery of transference for psychoanalysis. From that point on, the development of psychoanalysis both as a theory and as a practice rested on the elucidation of the transference.

Recognizing the transference meant that it was no longer necessary to use the force of suggestion to persuade the patient of the reality of his repressed impulses. Freud could point out in real time how these impulses were coming to life in the patient's current relationship with the analyst. Suggestion could at last be discarded. There is a real question, however, whether Freud availed himself of the opportunity to do so. He seems instead to have used his discovery of the transference not to discard suggestion altogether, but to devise a new form of it that was at once more subtle and more powerful than the old one.

One aspect of the newly discovered transference was what he called the positive transference, and one manifestation of the positive transference was an unconscious infantile wish to be cured by a powerful parent in a quasi-magical way. Freud viewed the positive transference as a repetition of the patient's childhood relationship to a trusted and loved parent. Instead of seizing the opportunity that the discovery of transference had given him to interpret this repressed, infantile aspect of the patient's personality in an impartial and even-handed way, Freud interpreted the transference selectively: he interpreted only the aspects of the transference that threatened the patient's cooperative attitude—the hostile or frankly erotic ones—leaving untouched the positive and affectionate ones. The reason he gave for this was that the positive transference was necessary to motivate the patients to do the painful work of overcoming his repression and acknowledging his impulses, which he would presumably do out of love for the analyst-parent. He would remember what the analyst wanted him to remember because the analyst wanted him to, and because the patient loved him a childlike way and wanted to please him the way a child wants to please his parents.[7]

The positive transference is one of the two legs (along with a certain type of countertransference) on which suggestion stands. It renders the patient highly susceptible to the analyst's power of suggestion, because he and the analyst with whom he is in love now constitute a group of two functioning in basic assumption mode, in which emotional and mental synchrony is prominent at the expense of independent critical thought or what Malloch and Trevarthen called "discretizing".[8]

In this situation, it was now no longer necessary for the analyst to pressure or insist, or indeed even to suggest directly anything to the patient about what he needed to be conscious of. It was enough to use words (along, of course, with the music of speech) to gently guide the patient. The patient's susceptibility to suggestion depended on his childlike belief in the analyst's superior knowledge and wisdom. His idealization of the analyst caused him to respond strongly to even the subtlest of hints that he was being a "good patient", moving in the right direction, and therefore worthy of the analyst's love, (or conversely a "bad" one not so moving and not so worthy).

Freud's discussion of the transference in his paper on "The Dynamics of Transference" (1912) illuminates this new technique. He recognized that the positive transference itself was a creature of the very repressed childhood impulses and wishes that the analysis was intended to have the patient acknowledge and judge in a mature and sober way, but he was careful not to question, and thus possibly undermine, the positive transference in the analysis until it had served its purpose of motivating the patient to face his repressed impulses out of love for the parent/analyst. At the conclusion of the analysis, the positive transference would presumably either fall of its own weight, or finally be addressed and resolved directly by interpretation (although it was never clear exactly how this crucial final step, which Freud treated almost as an afterthought, was to transpire).

By advocating that one interpret the erotic or hostile transference that worked against the analyst's ability to practise suggestion, but leave untouched the positive, affection transference that supported it, Freud was advocating the use of interpretation not in the service of an open and disinterested exploration of the patient's mind—not an exploration of the patient's past and present wishes and fantasies, and how they influence the patient's character, illness, and perception of events. He was recommending a tendentious technique the purpose of which was to counteract and nullify certain kinds of transference in order to preserve the kind that gave Freud the power of suggestion over the patient. Freud used his discovery of the transference to practise suggestion in a way that was more sophisticated and subtle than Bernheim ever dreamed of. In a telling passage, he acknowledges this, but follows his acknowledgement with an attempt to distinguish what he was doing from ordinary suggestion:

> we readily admit that the results of psycho-analysis rest upon suggestion; by suggestion, however, we must understand the influencing of a person by means of the transference phenomena which are possible in his case. We take care of the patient's final independence by employing suggestion in order to get him to accomplish a piece of psychical work which has as its necessary result a permanent improvement in his psychical situation.
> *(Freud, 1912, pp. 105–106)*

Thanks to Freud's work, we now know that the power of suggestion rests entirely on the transference relationship.[9] This means that, "influencing of a person by means of the transference phenomena which are possible in his case" is simply an unrestricted definition of suggestion and a description of how it works in every case. Freud couches his definition of suggestion in terms that make it appear that he is talking about something different—narrower—than ordinary suggestion.

When he writes, "We take care of the patient's final independence by employing suggestion in order to get him to accomplish a piece of psychical work which has as its necessary result a permanent improvement in his psychical situation", he is presumably referring to the fact that he employs suggestion in the service of de-repression. We may ask, however, about the fate of one piece of repressed psychic material in particular: the unconscious transference to the analyst as the trusted parent of childhood that forms the basis of the patient's suggestibility and also places him in the psychological position of a child vis-à-vis the analyst. Note that this is not the same as the analyst being in fact a concerned, attentive doctor, and the patient appreciating him in a realistic way, one adult to another. If that were the case, we would not be talking about transference or suggestion at all. Realistic adults believe things because there is evidence for them, not simply because they are suggested by a nice man that one wishes in a child-like way to please out of love (or, although Freud did not emphasize this, out of fear). Does the analyst in the end interpret the positive transference that had formed the basis of his therapeutic power? Does he disillusion the patient of this one last illusion? And if so, how does the patient react to the news that his kindly analyst has been seducing and manipulating him—there really seems to be no other way to describe it—all along? Would he not have to re-examine everything he had come to believe from the analysis? The analyst, could, in his defence, argue that all he had seduced the patient into doing was to see the truth about himself, and this is an unmitigated good for the patient. But in that case, why bother—why use suggestion in the first place? Presumably Freud supposed that the patient is not capable (at least for a long time) of recognizing the value of truth, and so he argued that the analyst has no choice but to circumvent this disability of the patient by using suggestion, albeit a kinder, gentler form than Bernheim's.

The relationship between psychoanalysis, suggestion, and truth in Freud's thinking is complex. His discovery of transference as the basis of suggestion allowed him to step back from the latter, and, having distanced himself, to see it from a new and extraordinarily fruitful perspective. This created the possibility of engaging the patient in a way that was quite distinct from the ancient tradition of suggestion. But while he opened this doorway, he did not in the end step through it. He appears to have analysed the transference only selectively, interpreting only those aspects of it that would interfere with the patient's "cooperation" in the analysis, but leaving untouched those that promoted it.[10]

Freud's decision to use the transference to motivate the patient to "overcome his repression"—that is, as a tool for suggestion—instead of treating it as a living source of information about what was being repressed is baffling. If transference is repetition that replaces remembering, then de-repression has already happened in everything but word. What is transpiring in the analytic relationship (being acted out) merely needs to be observed and described. Evidently, Freud did not believe that the patient's need to learn the truth would carry him through. He opted to control the patient's state of mind by exploiting the patient's love for the analyst, rather than trust the patient's ability to freely learn the truth (at least in the long run). The analyst's need to control the patient's mind in this way is the analyst's countertransference—based on his need to see himself as a healer (as opposed to a guide). This countertransference is the second leg on which suggestion stands. Together with the patient's positive transference, it forms a basic assumption belief system that seems to guarantee that a "cure" will be delivered by a powerful and benevolent parent/analyst to a helpless child/patient. But here Freud struck a Faustian bargain that left him in a dangerous position.

For example, Freud's rationale—that he was only using suggestion as a stopgap to help the patient learn the truth about himself—raises the question of what truth is, and who is to decide when the patient is reaching it in the course of the analysis. In principle, the patient is free to decide for himself that the analysis has served its purpose. But given the perennial difficulty of arriving at a truly candid and complete assessment of oneself, the patient's assessment of himself must always be suspect. Freud's use of suggestion to induce the patient to recognize the truth about his unconscious is, of course, worlds away from Bernheim's use of suggestion to suppress symptoms directly. But it is also worlds away from engaging the patient as an equal in a joint and open-ended exploration of his mind.

The analyst's use of suggestion as a way of shepherding the patient towards the truth not only places the patient in the psychological position of a dependent child, it forces the analyst into the role of what Lacan called "*le sujet supposé savoir*" (the one who is supposed to know). The analyst is forced to play the authority. His exploitation of the positive transference defines his role in the analysis as inevitably as it defines that of the patient.

The positive transference is a mode of human bonding that lends itself to the type of basic assumption belief that Bion called "dependency". In this case, the analyst is the nominal leader of a group of two founded on the basic assumption that it is being led by an omniscient god—"one who knows". The leader of a group functioning in the basic assumption mode is as restricted by the basic assumption as any other group member. He must live up to his role in the basic assumption fantasy or risk losing his authority.

Here the basic assumption comes into conflict with the realities of the analytic situation. If the analyst is supposed to know the truth about the patient, how is he supposed to know it? This now becomes a question of paramount importance, not only clinically, but ethically as well. The use of suggestion to lead the patient to the truth means that the clinical and ethical integrity of the analysis depends entirely on the analyst's version of the truth being true. But of course, there is no way of assuring that this is so. There is no guarantee that the analyst's immunity to subjective bias is firm enough to carry this burden. The irony implicit in Lacan's phrase is that the analyst is a subject who is supposed to "know" objectively. Faced with this impossible dilemma, the analyst in practice (or more precisely, the analyst practising suggestion) eventually resorts to psychoanalytic theory—the accumulated wisdom of his professional group—that he hopes will provide him with the needed objectivity. But this crowdsourcing merely shifts the burden of "knowing" from the individual analyst to the group's theories, and their truth now becomes absolutely critical to the success and ethical integrity of the whole analysis.

But which group's theories? Since Freud's death eighty years ago, psychoanalysis has become increasingly complex and Balkanized. This is not necessarily a bad thing, despite the attendant strife and controversy, but it raises serious questions about whether any group's theories are indisputable enough to carry the responsibility that practising members of the group must place on them.

This dubiousness is especially true of psychoanalytic theory, because, as every scientist knows, scientific theories, especially theories in a field as young and turbulent as psychoanalysis, can be only tentative and must retain their malleability under the impact of new observation.[11] The requirement that psychoanalytic theory be true in the way needed by psychoanalysts who use suggestion is too great a burden for even a highly robust theory to bear, let alone psychoanalytic theory in its present state of development, where malleability is so crucial. Under the crushing weight of this contradiction, psychoanalytic theories that need to be fluid, scientific conjectures (tentative hypotheses about reality) become compressed into rigid dogma (something to believe in order to achieve a sense of certainty).[12]

The generations of psychoanalysts who succeeded Freud have found themselves caught in this contradiction. One can see the tendency towards the ossification of theory into dogma at the institutional level (under the banner of "scientific rigor") by comparing two definitions of psychoanalysis.[13] The first is Freud's, written in 1913:

> Psychoanalysis is a medical procedure which aims at the cure of certain forms of nervous disease (the neuroses) by a psychological technique.[14]

The second, from 2001, is a definition of psychoanalysis found in the statutes of the International Psychoanalytic Association:

> The term psychoanalysis refers to a theory of personality structure and function and to a specific psycho-therapeutic technique. This body of knowledge is based on and derived from the fundamental psychological discoveries made by Sigmund Freud.[15]

In the interval of ninety years between these two definitions, psychoanalysis seems to have been transformed from an investigative psychological procedure into a theory of personality structure to which a specific psychotherapeutic technique is subservient. Psychoanalysis is now "based on and derived from" Freud's psychological discoveries, acting as a fixed foundation and source of knowledge for psychoanalysis. This reverses the priorities of real science, which is based on investigative technique—certain procedures for gathering and assessing evidence—as a source of knowledge, about which one may theorize in any number of ways, as long as the theories remain subservient to the data. The ultimate legacy of Freud's failure to abandon suggestion decisively has been to leave psychoanalysts in a highly ambiguous position *vis-à-vis* their theories, saddled with the burden of having to adopt dogma while at the same time retaining the flexibility needed to see what is unique and unexpected about each patient. Their response to this challenge has been less than completely successful.[16]

Is it possible to answer this challenge in a more successful way? Is it possible to do psychoanalysis without relying on the power of suggestion and the positive transference to convince patients of theories that may, in the end, turn out to be little more than dogma? In other words, is it possible for psychoanalysis to finally break clearly and definitively free from suggestion?

Notes

1 See in this connection "Does Psychoanalysis Heal? A Contribution to the Theory of Psychoanalytic Technique" (Caper, 1992).
2 He also had other reasons to abandon this theory: by his calculation, based on the prevalence of hysteria among middle class Viennese women, sexual molestation of middle class children would have had to have been nearly universal. In addition, his self-analysis indicated that, if his theory were correct, he would himself have had to have been molested as a child. He considered both of these possibilities too unlikely to maintain. Most importantly, he found that "there are no indications of reality in the unconscious, so that one cannot distinguish between truth and fiction that had been cathected with affect [i.e. emotion-laden fantasies]" (Freud, 1985, pp. 264–265).
3 The fact that the results of the cathartic technique were only temporary counted against it, of course, but only in the way that the often temporary results of cancer chemotherapy count against it.
4 Although the shift from the molestation theory to the theory of unconscious fantasy produced little immediate alteration in Freud's therapeutic technique, it was an extremely important shift in his theoretical thinking, as later developments would show.
5 Strikingly for the modern reader, Freud at first regarded repression to be a pathological mechanism and its product, the unconscious, to be a pathological formation found only in hysterical illness. Non-hysterics presumably did not practise repression and did not have an unconscious.
6 "The past is never dead. It's not even past."
7 Freud's famous dictum that psychoanalysis was a cure through love did not mean, as it is sometimes misunderstood, that it was the analyst's love for the patient that cures. It means that the patient is cured through his love for the analyst.
8 The lack of critical thought about the loved object is not peculiar to the analytic relationship: it is characteristic of being in love in general.
9 As he put it, "there remains as a definition for suggestion: a conviction which is not based upon perception and reasoning but upon an erotic tie" (Freud, 1921, p. 127).
10 I put quote marks around "cooperation" because there is a real question whether someone who is being groomed and massaged for suggestion could be said to be truly cooperating.
11 For a further discussion of this, see Chapter 7, "Psychoanalysis and Science" below.
12 This may be the reason why debates between contending psychoanalytic theories and groups tend eventually to take on the qualities of religious wars, complete with anathematization and excommunication (see, for example, Kirsner 2000).
13 I am indebted to Giovanni Vassalli for pointing this out in the *International Journal of Psychoanalysis* (Vassalli, 2001).
14 "The Claims of Psychoanalysis to Scientific Interest" *SE* 13, p. 165.
15 IPA Membership Handbook and Roster 2001, p. 27, Article 3.
16 The classical form of dogmatism has the analyst as an authority whose pronouncements are not to be seriously challenged. More recently, a new form of dogmatism

has appeared in psychoanalysis, in which the patient's pronouncements are not to be challenged. For example, if the patient feels hurt or misunderstood by the analyst, then it must be assumed that the analyst has hurt or misunderstood him, however inadvertently, and something like an an apology is in order to "repair the breach in trust". While this may indeed be in order, to assume that it is so without investigation is simply the old authoritarian dogmatism with the polarity reversed.

Bibliography

Joseph Breuer and Sigmund Freud. Studies on hysteria. *The Standard Edition of the Complete Psychological Works of Sigmund Freud*, 2, 1895.

Robert Caper. Does psychoanalysis heal? A contribution to the theory of psychoanalytic technique. *The International Journal of Psycho-Analysis*, 73:283–292, 1992. Reprinted in *A Mind of One's Own*, Routledge, 1999, pp. 19–31.

Sigmund Freud. Project for a scientific psychology. *The Standard Edition of the Complete Psychological Works of Sigmund Freud*, 1:281–391, 1895.

Sigmund Freud. The dynamics of transference. *The Standard Edition of the Complete Psychological Works of Sigmund Freud*, 12:99–108, 1912.

Sigmund Freud. Group psychology and the analysis of the ego. *The Standard Edition of the Complete Psychological Works of Sigmund Freud*, 18:69–143, 1921.

Sigmund Freud. *The Complete Letters of Sigmund Freud to Wilhelm Fliess 1887–1904*, Translated and edited by J. M. Masson. Harvard University Press, Cambridge, MA, 1985.

Douglas Kirsner. *Unfree Associations: Inside Psychoanalytic Institutes*. Process Press, London, 2000.

Giovanni Vassalli. The birth of psychoanalysis from the spirit of technique. *The International Journal of Psycho-Analysis*, 82:3–25, 2001.

5
PSYCHOANALYSIS BEYOND SUGGESTION

Suggestion relies on a combination of seduction (playing on the patient's desire to be loved) and intimidation (playing on the patient's fear of being spurned or rejected). In both cases, the analyst is taking advantage of the parental role assigned to him in the patient's transference. Playing the parental role means that the analyst is passing judgement on how "good" or "bad" the patient is being, as though the patient were a child.

While very few if any analysts will endorse praise or condemnation as good psychoanalytic technique, and all will maintain that they do not practise it, this seems to be true only of the analyst's conscious, verbal communications to the patient. In recent years, the International Psychoanalytic Association has sponsored research into how its members actually work (as distinct from their conscious beliefs about how they work). The Comparative Clinical Method study gathers a group of analysts together to scrutinize in minute detail the work of one member of the group. This has revealed that, although the analyst consciously believes he is implementing one theory of psychoanalytic interpretation and treatment, his actual interpretations may imply quite a different theory. In other words, the analyst may have unconscious theories about the nature of psychoanalytic work that have an impact on what he actually does far greater than his conscious theories.

The unconscious, musical register of communication (for example, tone of voice) is undoubtedly a more important vehicle of suggestion than the conscious semantic-verbal register. If we examine the musical register, we may find a picture quite different from that of the verbal content of which the analyst is aware. Most instances of suggestion are conveyed not by overt communication, but by shadings of song-and-dance intonation and phrasing subtle enough to escape the analyst's attention unless focussed upon.

Obviously, the analyst may avoid practising suggestion by refusing to play the role of parent, praising or condemning the patient, however subtly—and instead merely observing how things are with the patient, without value judgement or suggestions. This is far easier said than done, for two reasons. The first is the analyst's countertransference, which is by definition unconscious and which, if it contains a desire to heal or cure the patient, will inevitably (and unconsciously) lead into some practice of suggestion as a means of forcing a "cure" when the analyst encounters resistance. The second reason is the patient's transference, which, if it contains the desire to be in the presence of an all-powerful healer (god), will join with the analyst's countertransference to form a *folie à deux* powerful enough to undermine any conscious desire to avoid suggestion.

While it may in principle be possible for the analyst to avoid verbal judgements and suggestions by carefully monitoring and controlling what he says, it is far more difficult for him to control the musical elements of his speech, which are largely unconscious and involuntary. Subtle differences in tone, timing, rhythm, verbal connotation and body language will all betray his unconscious intentions.[1] For the analyst to avoid practising suggestion, he must overcome his need for it, which means abandoning its promise to heal the patient. He must accept in his depths that it is not his job to solve the patient's problems, direct the patient along the road to health, or eliminate his pain. Psychoanalysis does not heal. It is a much more modest art that perhaps only sheds light on self-deception. Furthermore, even if the analysis is successful in this, there is no guarantee that exposing self-deception will either solve the problems the patient wants solved or immunize him from painful realizations.

This renunciation involves a radical rejection of many of the ideas that we may have about psychoanalysis. Foremost among these is the idea that psychoanalysis either directly remedies some psychological deficit or directly corrects some derangement in the patient's mental functioning. Psychoanalysis does neither of these. Treatment by suggestion, on the other hand, promises precisely such a cure.

"Curing" has two components: one is relief of pain and the other is removal of the underlying cause of the pain. If a putative cure fails to eliminate pain (which psychoanalysis may well do), it is subject to criticism as a failed cure (even more so if it actually produces new pains, which psychoanalysis may also do). Likewise, if a supposed cure fails to remove the cause of the problem, it is subject to the same criticism. Some of the criticism to which psychoanalysis has been subjected is due to this misunderstanding about what it is and what it can do. If psychoanalysis were to be a cure in this sense—focussed directly on the removal of pain and on removing the cause of the problem—then it would have to commit itself to shaping the patient's mind in a certain way—that is, it would have to stop being what it is and fall back into the practice of suggestion.

Removing psychoanalysis from the sphere of suggestion would then seem to require that it give up the idea that it is intended to produce a cure. Re-orienting it towards something like a search for truth about the patient, disregarding how "therapeutic", non-"therapeutic" or even anti-"therapeutic" this may be by conventional standards of cure, reveals the truly radical nature of psychoanalysis, and the vastness of the gap between the goals of psychoanalysis, on one hand and those of medical treatment such as psychiatry and psychological treatment such as behavioural therapy, on the other. Re-oriented in this way, the analyst's aim shifts away from "therapy" towards the more modest goals of observation and description, and in place of "cure", the more modest goal of psychological development. Psychoanalysis does not cure; it only illuminates.

Perhaps most importantly, detaching analysis from the need to cure allows it to stand back from and to study the practice it would otherwise be engaged in as a means of cure, namely suggestion. Suggestion is a two-way street. It is a type of basic assumption activity, which means that both participants—analyst and patient—must tacitly participate in it. The analyst, for his part, is motivated by his need to heal or cure the patient. The patient, for his part, is motivated by the congruent need to be healed or cured. This means that both agree that the patient is a child in need of guidance and correction in life, and that the analyst is just the parent to do it. This basic assumption idea is unconscious, and the main vehicle through which it is conveyed and maintained is the register of song-and-dance, operating below the radar. Each participant is not only playing a role according to his unconscious needs; he is also drafting the other into the necessary complementary role. The analyst playing the role of parent drafts the patient into the role of child, and the patient playing the role of child drafts the analyst into the role of parent.

The analyst who restricts his activity to observations about what is transpiring in the analysis is in a position to make observations about the patient's drafting him into the role of an approving or disapproving parent. And prominent among his observations of this transference are observations about the forces transmitted in the register of song-and-dance. These forces, which exert pressure on the analyst to behave in a way that realizes the patient's transference—might be described as the patient's practice of suggestion on the analyst.[2]

As a practice of non-suggestion, the analysis is able to focus on the forces that underlie suggestion as they are active in the analytic session. To the degree that suggestion is really abandoned as a means of treatment and cure, attention may directed towards the workings of unconscious song-and-dance that produce basic assumption mentality as the basis of suggestion. The questions that come to the fore are then what is being sung and danced, and what are the anxieties that drive it (and necessarily prevent critical thought about it as a basic assumption activity). These anxieties are the forces that drive one to practise and desire "curing" through suggestion, and shedding light on the song-and-dance vehicle of suggestion constitutes the analysis of suggestion.

In a successful analysis, the patient's motive for analytic work gradually shifts away from the infantile wish to please or ingratiate oneself to an all-wise and all-powerful parent, towards a realistic, adult desire to know the truth about oneself in order to become more sane. Growth, and development, even at the cost of mental pain and social difficulties, now replace the wish to be cured of painful states. The value that shapes psychoanalysis in this new orientation is not cure, but truth.

Suggestion and interpretation

The psychoanalytic method is the foundation of psychoanalysis, and it is possible to identify at least some of what constitutes the specifically psychoanalytic method—what makes psychoanalysis revolutionary—by contrasting it with its pre-revolutionary predecessor, suggestion.

What distinguishes psychoanalysis from suggestion and its latter-day variants, behavioural therapy and supportive psychotherapy, is that, while the latter utilize the transference to shape or mould the patient's mind (encouraging the positive transference and discouraging the negative transference), psychoanalysis explores the transference in as even-handed a way as possible (neither encouraging nor discouraging any of its manifestations), with the intent of putting into perspective (through understanding) the forces on which suggestion and supportive psychotherapy rely, whether they are used deliberately as a "therapeutic" technique, or occur unwittingly in what is known as enactment. This is psychoanalytic interpretation.

The therapeutic use of suggestion is inseparable from ideas of pathology and treatment. Suggestion is a tool used to mould the patient's mind into a shape that the therapist regards as less abnormal, in the same way that a physician will try to reduce a patient's cholesterol level to a less pathological state. This deliberate use of suggestion is usually called supportive psychotherapy. What supportive psychotherapy supports are trends in the patient's mental and emotional life that the therapist regards as bringing the patient closer to normal mental functioning. "Support" also means discouraging trends in the patient's mind that would move him in the opposite direction. This support may be conveyed by words, or by tone of voice and timing, or by body language—the currency of song-and-dance. Support is a systematic attempt to get the patient to think or feel in a certain way. Supportive psychotherapy acts by exploiting the positive transference through song-and-dance, while psychoanalysis acts by exploring that very activity. One consequence of this is that supportive psychotherapy, far from being a less intense derivative of psychoanalysis, as it is often regarded, is in fact incompatible with psychoanalysis. One may do one or the other, but not both at the same time.

Enactments and interpretation

Even when psychoanalysts do not deliberately engage in suggestion or support, they may do so unintentionally and unwittingly. The unintentional use of suggestion is called enactment, and is of great interest to psychoanalysts precisely because it is not deliberate: it is the product of complex unconscious interactions present in the relationship between patient and analyst. These enactments consist partly of behaviour (both verbal and non-verbal) that has as its effect the creation of a state of mind in another person that corresponds to the subject's wishes and fantasies for that person. These kinds of enactments are attempts to bring the reality of other people's minds into line with one's fantasies and wishes for them. Seduction and intimidation, to the degree that they are unconscious, are not only the tools of suggestion, they are the tools of enactments. While these phenomena obviously occur quite commonly in everyday life, they are not often studied in detail: psychoanalysis gives us a chance to study them carefully. They are biopsies of the live unconscious, and give patient and analyst a valuable opportunity to study it in the flesh.

Patients and analysts both engage in enactments. The patient acts in certain ways in an attempt to mold the analyst into the shape that the patient needs him to be, and the analyst, when he is enacting something, is also (unconsciously) trying to mould the patient to fit his needs and desires. Part of the analyst's job is to describe the enactments as they occur. He could be called a reporter—someone who observes and describes—if his reports are understood to include his own participation in the events he describes. The analyst can observe his own participation in enactment only to the extent that his countertransference need to be a healer has been analysed and worked through in his own analysis.

Enactments are such important material for the analyst because they reflect in real time the unconscious emotional forces active in the analysis—the waking dream lives of both participants and the products of their intersection. A timely description of these forces, as they are happening, gives both participants in the analysis a chance to judge for themselves how apt (or otherwise) the description (interpretation) is before what is being described has flown the stage: the patient's question to the analyst, "how do you know that?" or "why do you say that?", can be answered by pointing to emotional experiences that are still alive at the time. Psychoanalysis now has the chance to go beyond suggestion and persuasion to live observation and assessment.

Notes

1 "He that has eyes to see and ears to hear may convince himself that no mortal can keep a secret. If his lips are silent, he chatters with his finger-tips; betrayal oozes out of him at every pore" (Freud, 1905, p. 77).
2 In practice, the analyst's vulnerability to these suggestions from the patient varies in proportion to the degree to which the analyst is using suggestion against the patient.

Bibliography

Sigmund Freud. Fragment of an analysis of a case of hysteria. *The Standard Edition of the Complete Psychological Works of Sigmund Freud*, 7:7–122, 1905.

6

THE ANALYST'S OEDIPAL DILEMMA

Introduction

In 1953, Wilfred Bion read a paper to a meeting of the International Psychoanalytic Association outlining his new theory of schizophrenia. He concluded with the following claim:

> if the course I have indicated above is followed there is reason to anticipate that the schizophrenic may achieve his own form of adjustment to reality which may be no less worthy of the title of "cure" because it is not of the same kind as that which is achieved by less disordered patients.

Upon republication of this paper 15 years later, he added an appendix which, remarkably, did not just back away from his claim of having found a psychoanalytic cure for schizophrenia, but questioned the whole idea of psychoanalysis as a cure for anything at all:

> When I wrote this section I had not appreciated the extent to which ideas of cure ... pervaded not only psycho-analysis but the whole domain of mental or spiritual life ... the religious approach to the domains of mental life activates the apparatus of expectation of "cure" of "painful" emotions and experiences in a way which would be appropriate to physical pain associated with physical relief and physical therapeutic measures ... [such] expectations ... could be summed up: "There is a pain. It should be removed. Someone must remove it forthwith. preferably by magic or omnipotence or omniscience, and at once; failing that by science" ... [in consequence] a sharpened awareness of painful emotional experiences would be a mark against the approach, scientific or religious, which was responsible. The psycho-analyst himself can act as if he embraced this

view. It offers a simpler explanation and justification for the expense in time and money of psychoanalysis. Without it psycho-analysis becomes an activity which is hard to justify. Furthermore, it provides psychoanalyst and analysand with a "memory" which gives both the sense of security that comes from a feeling that they are not engaged on any activity new to the human group.

(Bion, 1967, p. 149)

He goes on to mention his now-familiar idea of the container and the contained, pointing out that there is always a tension between the two, and that this tension is also found in the relationship between an idea and the statements used to express (or, as he would say, contain) it. An example of this tension is the relationship between psychoanalysis itself and the language with which we try to conceptualize it:

Any formulation of it, or person entertaining it, or group (such as a psycho-analytical society) harbouring it, will show evidence of that stress. The abandonment of a protective shell of familiar ideas will expose the person or group who abandons it to the disruptive (even if creative) force of the "contained" idea. Therefore "memory" is kept in constant repair as a defensive barrier. Prominent amongst these "memories" in a psycho-analytical Society is the idea of cure … The psycho-analyst must not be surprised to find he is himself as unwilling as his analysand, or his group, to abandon the desire for cure or its idea. Nor can abandonment be achieved by an act of will. It is a short step from abandonment of "cure" to the discovery of the reality of psycho-analysis and the unfamiliarity of the world of psycho-analytical experience. The "desire" for cure is one example of precisely the desire that must, in common with all desires, not be entertained by a psychoanalyst. The reader will find evidence in these papers that though I had suspected I had not grasped the importance of this point.

(Bion, 1967, pp. 151–152)

Psychoanalysis and truth

In reconsidering his earlier claim, Bion was urging us to question our assumptions about psychoanalysis and the words we use to describe it—even, or perhaps especially, those that seem most obvious. Because psychoanalysis is such a radically new enterprise, old terms are as likely to obscure its true nature as to reveal it. If we accept Bion's suggestion that we question whether psychoanalysis is a form of treatment that offers some kind of cure, we are left with the obvious question: if not that, what is it—what does it do? His answer is that it points to the truth, and does nothing else. This response is as remarkable for what it rules out as for what it rules in. It means that psychoanalysis does not try to improve that patient's personality, or diminish any kind of illness, nor does it aim to relieve suffering or make the patient more agreeable, successful or capable. It aims at one thing only: to hold up a mirror in which the patient might recognize himself.

An interpretation is merely the analyst's attempt to call it like he sees it. Or almost that. Since an interpretation is an attempt to communicate something, it must be tactful; a patient who is too upset by what he is hearing will not be able to hear it, and it will fail as a communication. The only other caveat is that the analyst must refer in his interpretation to some evidence that both he and the patient are able to see, so the patient can form an independent judgement about the validity of the analyst's use of evidence. This brings up a related point: in Bion's view, psychoanalysis is an activity between two equal and independent adults. The analyst talks about various layers of the patient's personality, including infantile parts, but the analyst is talking to the other adult in the room. He is not trying to reassure or re-parent a frightened child; he is trying to enlighten a curious adult.

In *A Memoir of the Future*, Bion says that "the nearest that the psychoanalytic couple comes to a 'fact' is when one or the other has a feeling" (Bion, 1990, pp. 150–151). Feelings are the raw data on which psychoanalysis relies to arrive at whatever truths it can arrive at. To put this more directly, psychoanalysis aims at whatever truths may be arrived at by starting with the feelings that arise in the patient or the analyst during application of the psychoanalytic method (free association, evenly-hovering attention, non-judgmental exploration of what arises in the session, respect for the unconscious, and so on).

In Bion's view, the nature of the psychoanalytic process forces the psychoanalyst along one of two paths, and he must make a stark choice between them. He may either pursue non-tendentiously the kind of truth that psychoanalysis is uniquely able to discover by communicating observations derived from psychoanalytic "facts"—meaning, ultimately, the only facts of which he can be certain, his own emotional experience in the psychoanalytic session—and doing nothing else. To the degree that he deviates from this narrow path, he finds himself on the other: the path of tendentious psychological manipulation. In this case, he is doing something close to the opposite of pursuing the truth: he is behaving like the enemy of truth, a propagandist who "works on his public's emotions with an end in view and … does not intend his public to be free in its choice of the use to which it puts the communication he makes" (Bion, 1965, p. 37).

The analyst contributing to a search for truth can only communicate his observations, and cannot try to shape the patient's mind "therapeutically" because as a psychoanalyst he does "not aim to run the patient's life but [only] to enable him to run it according to his lights and therefore to know what his lights are". Furthermore, his communication to the patient must be limited so that it "express[es] truth without any implication other than the implication that it is true in the analyst's opinion" (Bion, 1965, p. 37), because if the analyst suggests that his words are any more than his own opinion, that is, based on his own subjective experience, he is departing from his role as observer of psychoanalytic fact (foremost among which are his subjective experiences). He is also investing his communications with an authority that places them somehow above the patient's own observations, an authority that transforms his communication from a modest observation about his own experience into propaganda about a "superior" way for the patient to think about himself.

The psychoanalyst who makes clear that he is simply communicating his experience or his take on things invites the patient to think critically about what he is saying. In fact, Bion urges us to make sure the patient never loses sight of the fact that the analyst is only expressing an opinion. He rather insists that the patient think critically about what he is saying. By sticking to facts in this way, the analyst contributes to the patient's understanding.

The psychoanalyst (or psychotherapist) acting in a therapeutic mode is acting as a propagandist to lead the patient to a predetermined point. He may be concerned with the emotional facts of the session, but if so, this concern is not paramount; he does not want the patient to think critically about what he says; he merely wants to shape the patient's experience.

Since it is not possible to shape something while at the same time respecting its natural shape, this "therapeutic" endeavour flourishes at the expense of an exploration of the truth.

The dichotomy that Bion is urging is between communication of the analyst's own experience of the patient without regard to consequences—what he calls a search for truth—and communication that regards nothing *but* its consequences—what he calls propaganda. The dichotomy hinges on the analyst's intent (unconscious as well as conscious) while communicating to the patient. The importance of the analyst avoiding desire is apparent once we realize that the practice of suggestion is an expression of the analyst's desire for the patient; he is trying to shape the patient's mind into what he wants it to be (even when his desire for the patient is, from a certain point of view, "altruistic"). It is, of course, impossible for the analyst to avoid desire altogether, since it arises from his unconscious, over which he has no control. What he can do is cultivate his capacity to be aware of the (inevitable) intrusion of his own desires into his analytic work, and treat them as grist for the psychoanalytic mill. This converts his desires from an intrusion into a valuable source of information about what is transpiring at the moment in the psychoanalytic relationship.

A psychoanalytic dilemma

The need and desire for truth is an expression of the desire to know oneself, one's objects and the world in general (this is what Bion called "K"). This need to know follows from love for these things. The pursuit of truth, however, conflicts with another need: the need for security.[2] With this dilemma in mind, Bion proposed a reading of the Oedipus myth that focusses not on what Freud emphasized—Oedipus's murder of his father and incestuous relationship with his mother—but on his thirst for knowledge in the face of any danger, as indicated by his boldness in risking his life to answer the riddle of the Sphinx and in ignoring the dire warnings of the blind Tiresias against pursuing his investigation into the source of the plague devastating his city of Thebes. If we read the myth in this way, it becomes a story that points directly to the dilemma posed by the psychoanalyst's single-minded commitment to a search for truth.

When Oedipus, King of Thebes, learned of the oracle's message that the plague that was devastating his city was the result of an offense against the gods, he swore to seek out the source of the offense. The blind seer Tiresias warned him that in doing so he was endangering himself by committing the sin of hubris—the overweening pride that drives a mortal to think he can mix in affairs reserved for the gods.

Despite this, Oedipus pressed on relentlessly until he identified the offense, which, as Tiresias had warned, came at the cost of revealing a truth so unacceptable that it precipitated his ostracism from Thebes, his self-mutilation, and his mother's suicide. This terrible misfortune seemed like the nemesis that validated Tiresias's warning that, by undertaking his investigations, Oedipus was committing an act of hubris.

The Oedipus myth has a counterpart in the myth of the Garden of Eden, where Jehovah plays the role of Tiresias, warning that partaking of the fruit of the tree of knowledge will lead only to destruction. While it is true that Adam and Eve's disobedience does bring death into the world, it also brings sexual creativity—in other words, life. By disobeying Jehovah's prohibition, the couple escaped a state that was neither alive nor dead. It may not be a coincidence that Tiresias was also punished by a god for committing a sin connected with sexuality. In various versions of the myth, he was blinded for revealing the secrets of the gods (parents), for watching snakes copulate, for watching Aphrodite bathe, or for giving Hera the wrong answer when she asked him whether men or women enjoyed greater sexual pleasure.

In both the Oedipus myth and the Eden myth, what leads to punishment is the desire for knowledge.[3] The course of action the story warns us against—the single-minded pursuit of the truth—is precisely the one that the psychoanalyst needs to follow. For the patient who is blind to himself, as for the blind Tiresias, not looking is a way of avoiding disaster; but for the psychoanalyst, this self-inflicted blindness, the result of severing connections in the mind, is the disaster.

It is in the nature of discovery that one does not know what will be discovered beforehand, has no guarantee that one will be glad to have made the discovery, know beforehand where it will take him, or even ever understand what was discovered. As in the Oedipus myth, there is always the danger that exploration will bring to light a previously unsuspected catastrophe. What the myth portrays as the natural law of hubris and nemesis is a cautionary tale about the potentially catastrophic effects of discovery.

Discovery puts at risk our sense of security, and it does so in unpredictable ways. The motto of our need for security might be "knowledge up to the point it becomes disruptive, then tranquillity above all else". Because life's uncertainties undermine our sense of security, and because threats to our security can produce such violent emotions, we can sympathize with Tiresias's dread of discovering the truth. Only by blocking ideas that threaten the security of our view of ourselves and the world—by disconnecting them from the main part of one's mind—and then covering up the evidence of the disconnection (by a kind of self-mutilation of one's consciousness), can one save oneself from potential catastrophe. This is how repression and splitting look from the point of view of their advocates (and we are all their practitioners and advocates).

Despite the disasters that befell him, Oedipus, having wandered the earth in disgrace in the years following his discoveries, came in the end to have his humanity understood and forgiven and to achieve some shelter from his torment. At home at last in the grove of the Eumenides and among the citizens of Colonus, he died peacefully in a state of grace that was denied to those who spurned and scorned him.[4] He had achieved at harrowing cost what is rare among men and even rarer among the powerful: he was an honest man.

Psychoanalysis and propaganda

The distinction Bion drew between non-tendentious communication, which is intended to be thought about, and propaganda, which is to intended to be not thought about, but instead to circumvent thought and reflection, has a number of ramifications. Non-tendentious communications foster learning from experience. When the analyst communicates an observation that is based on his own experience, he is pointing to something in the hope that the patient will think about it and use it to increase his own understanding. Propaganda undermines learning from experience. The analyst employing propaganda intends, consciously or unconsciously, for the patient to be free only to arrive at whatever "understanding" (really misunderstanding) the propagandist intends him to have. Non-tendentious communication leaves the patient free to discover what he actually thinks, feels, and believes. It frees him to have thoughts that originate within his own experience. The propagandist intends to dominate another's mind precisely to prevent him from originating his own thoughts.

Although I have been discussing communication and propaganda in terms of the analyst's intent, what I have said also applies to the patient, who likewise seeks to shape the analyst's mind, for example to win his love, sympathy, approval and endorsement, or to dispel the analyst's hatred or disapproval of the patient. The same type of interaction can be found (though perhaps not as easily demonstrated) between any two people who are in emotional contact with each other. We all communicate with others, but we all also have an idea of how the people around us could be "improved" so as to make reaching our personal goals with them easier, and we all try to manipulate them in the hope of realizing the desired improvements. One of the virtues of psychoanalysis is that it enables one to discover this type of propagandizing as it occurs between people, and to understand the how and why of its operation. As I hope is clear from the preceding chapter, suggestion is an example of this propagandizing.

Clinical illustration

Here is an example taken from a supervised case. The analyst was an experienced psychotherapist who was treating his first analytic case under supervision. The patient was a businessman in his 40's who came to analysis because of chronic depression related to feelings of unbearable inferiority. After a period of analysis, it became apparent that his emotional life was dominated by envy and the defences against it: he viewed the world as a dog-eat-dog arena, in which he had to maintain a constant vigil against being exploited and triumphed over. He envied other men's sexual prowess, but became terrified if he felt that a woman was interested in him sexually, since he viewed a sexual relationship as a form of predation in which the woman could satisfy herself only by draining him and leaving him behind as an empty shell. These anxieties were related to his unconscious conviction that all relationships would eventually succumb to mutual destructive envy between the people involved.

At the same time, he suffered from terrible guilt in his dealings with others: he constantly worried that he was exploiting his employees (especially the female ones), which caused him to bend over backwards to be fair in his dealings with them, in a futile attempt to avoid the guilt. In his sessions, he tried desperately to be a "good" patient, but always felt that he was failing. In reality, his associations often did have an artificial, forced quality, as though he was trying hard to comply with an analytic "requirement" that he associate freely when he was not capable of any real spontaneity. This lack of spontaneity turned out to be connected to his feeling under terrible pressure because he felt that the analyst was enviously judging his associations, and always finding them wanting.

The session I wish to describe in some detail occurred on a Monday. The patient entered and told his analyst that he had just attended a pop psychology event known as a "Bradshaw Weekend", from which he had gained many valuable insights about his behaviour that he had not gotten in 4 years with the analyst. He proceeded to list a number of what seemed to be valid insights, all of which the analyst had communicated to him many times in the past. The patient did not acknowledge this, but spoke as though it had all come from his "Bradshaw Weekend".

Although feeling quite irritated and threatened, the analyst succeeded with considerable effort in restraining himself and appearing reasonable and accepting of the patient's having benefited from the weekend. The patient went on to speak of his desire to leave analysis soon, hoping, he said, that this would not hurt the analyst who had been "like a mother and father to me" over the years. He then spoke of his mother's reaction when he announced his desire to leave home: "there's a cliff, if you want to go jump off of it, go ahead". The patient went on to say that he felt like he had just gotten his MD degree (the analyst was a social worker) and hoped the analyst would be like a proud father, congratulate him and wish him well.

The patient had left the analyst with the feeling that his work was rather pathetic and slow compared to that of the Bradshaw organization, the success and effectiveness of which he found himself envying. He had briefly considered using this countertransference as the basis of an interpretation about the patient's sense of inadequacy vis-a-vis himself, his envy of the analyst's abilities, and his defending himself from them by projecting both into the analyst. But he rejected this idea (despite its consistency with what he knew about the patient's difficulties with envy, his tendency to project it, and the fact that the "Bradshaw" insights had all appeared in the analysis before) because he felt that it would have made the patient see him as a spoil-sport, enviously denying the patient's good weekend experience. The patient would interpret the analyst's interpretation as a confirmation that it was the analyst who was filled with envy, not himself. At the same time, he had the vague feeling that, by remaining silent on the matter, he was somehow prostituting himself by implicitly assenting to what the patient had said.

The patient had managed to mount an effective propaganda campaign, which received his chronic envy by making it seem that it was the analyst, not he, who felt inadequate and envious. And indeed that was the case, thanks to the patient's skilful use of projective identification as propaganda.

What prevented the analyst from recognizing the patient's propaganda for what it was? He was just beginning his study of psychoanalysis and was still working in a psychotherapy mode. I believe that what made him vulnerable to the patient's projective identification was his own desire to practise projective identification on the patient in the form of "therapy", by which I mean tendentiously bringing about an "improvement" in the patient's mind or personality through the "therapeutic" use of projective identification (which is a form of propagandizing). This prevents him from recognizing the patient's propagandizing of the therapist. It is only a short step from the therapist's recognizing the patient's use of projective identification for propaganda purposes to recognizing his own use of it for the same purpose. This recognition would be catastrophic for the psychotherapist, since he did not yet have a solid analytic identity and his therapeutic approach was consequently still based on "improving" the patient's mind through psychotherapy, which implies controlling it, which in turn implies the use of projective identification. The catastrophe would be recognizing the propagandistic foundation of the psychotherapeutic approach before he had developed a professional alternative.

The analyst's Oedipal dilemma and the pain of the aesthetic conflict

In his commentary on his 1953 paper on schizophrenia, Bion remarked that, under the aegis of curing suffering, "a sharpened awareness of painful emotional experiences would be a mark against the approach, scientific or religious, which was responsible". Donald Meltzer's notion of the aesthetic conflict implies such an approach. The first aesthetic object is what he calls the "ordinary beautiful devoted mother", the original prototype of what we encounter over and over in our life-long engagement with the beauty of the world. Even the most devoted ordinary mother, however, is inconstant. She comes and goes in a way that is difficult for her infant to understand, and gives rise to suspicion: is she the infant's Beatrice or his Belle Dame sans Merci, a source of strength and sustenance or a treacherous demon? Her elusive Giocanda smile is hard to read. Meltzer locates the inescapable conflict between adoration and suspicion close to the heart of the psychopathology we see in our consulting rooms:

> The psychopathology which we study and allege [sic] to treat has its primary basis in the flight from the pain of the aesthetic conflict. The impact of separation, of deprivation—emotional and physical, of physical illness, of Oedipal conflict—pregenital and genital, of chance events, of seductions and brutality, of indulgence and over-protection, of family disintegration, of the death of parents or siblings—all of these derive the core of their significance for the developmental process from their contribution as aspects of the underlying, fundamental process of avoidance of the impact of the beauty of the world, and of passionate intimacy with another human being. It is necessary for our understanding of our patients, for a sympathetic view of the hardness, coldness and brutality that repeatedly bursts through in the transference and countertransference, to recognize that conflict about the present object is prior in significance to the host of anxieties over the absent object.
>
> *(Meltzer and Williams, 1988, p. 29)*

We cure the suffering of the aesthetic conflict only by detaching ourselves from the beauty of the world—a form of psychological self-mutilation. Bion's K is fundamentally an engagement with the world, whose full beauty we feel only at the price of suffering (tolerating) our painful relationship to it in all its elusiveness.

In his theory of linking, Bion described three kinds of link—L, H and K—which stand, roughly, for love, hate and curiosity. All are passions, but the K-link is fundamentally different from the other two. We may see this if we examine the relationship of each to the aesthetic object. L, standing for love, is what one feels towards one aspect of this object—the beauty of the world, the prototype of which is the ordinary beautiful mother, as seen through the baby's eyes. It is what one wants to possess forever. H, standing for hate, is what one feels towards the other aspect of the aesthetic object, the Belle Dame sans Merci, originally the treacherous mother whose physical and mental absences and preoccupations break the baby's illusion of possessing her, and evoke suspicion of treachery bordering even in healthy babies on paranoia. This is an object one wants to be rid of forever. Both possession and riddance are forms of control.

K, in contrast, does not seem to involve a desire to control. K is not Freud's epistemophilic instinct, a mixture of scopophilia and sadism, or even Mrs Klein's epistemophilic instinct, originally the desire to know about the inside of the mother, the inscrutable zone of the aesthetic object, as a form of intelligence gathering, the ultimate goal of which is control and power over her. K is more detached than either Freud's or Klein's epistemophilia, unconcerned with power and control. K is concerned with loving truth for its own sake, even if painful, perhaps as well for the sake of the relief that knowing the truth brings from the confusion and paranoia that preceded it. The K impulse does not attempt to control what it is learning about; it is interested in how things look when one is *not* controlling them.

Meltzer recognized the unique role that the K-link plays in the psychoanalytic process (and presumably in psychological development as well) when he wrote that,

> The [possessive] lover is naked as Othello to the whisperings of Iago, but is rescued by the quest for knowledge, the K-link, the desire to know rather than to possess the object of desire. The K-link points to the value of the desire as itself the stimulus to knowledge, not merely as a yearning for gratification and control over the object. Desire makes it possible, even essential, to give the object its freedom ... For in the interplay of joy and pain, engendering the love (L) and hate (H) links of ambivalence, it is the quest for understanding (K-link) that rescues the relationship from impasse ...
> *(Meltzer and Williams, 1988, pp. 27–28)*

In the end, the desire for truth, or the quest for understanding, cuts the knot of ambivalence that we feel towards the beauty of the world with all its treacherous elusiveness, and leads us to opt in favour of suffering our engagement with it as it is.

Discussion

The analyst's ability to do psychoanalysis depends on his practising a disciplined, radical respect for truth. This means deciding to respect the patient's personality rather than trying to shape it into a more desirable form (however he might construe that). It means subordinating his desire for cure, improvement, security, or professional prestige to a commitment to faithfully describe his experience with the patient. This is an ethic of respecting the shape of what one finds enough to confine oneself to merely describing it, and to refrain from trying to re-shape or improve it.

Practising psychoanalysis—restricting oneself to making observations intended only as something for the patient to think about, and accept or reject as he sees fit—means putting oneself in a position where the entirety of one's work with a patient may come to nothing, owing to factors that are in the final analysis completely beyond one's control. One cannot deliberately bring about the outcome one desires in psychoanalysis, and what is perhaps worse, even trying to do so is antithetical to psychoanalytic work. The psychoanalyst can recognize the humbling realities of the psychoanalytic situation only if he does not need these realities to contribute to his importance (for example, as a healer), and only if he can tolerate realities that do not do so. He must recognize the inevitability of the realities he faces and his own unimportance compared to them.

"Let us endeavour to see things as they are," wrote Samuel Johnson,

> and then enquire whether we ought to complain. Whether to see life as it is, will give us much consolation, I know not; but the consolation which is drawn from truth if any there be, is solid and durable: that which may be derived from errour, must be, like its original, fallacious and fugitive.
>
> (Boswell, 1889, p. 263)

Notes

1 This god is similar to the object of worship in Marx's view of religion as an opiate that keeps people from recognizing the reality of their economic situation.
2 Note the similarity between the two sides of this dilemma and the two types of group functioning: the work group's need for truth (contact with reality) and the basic assumption group's need for security.
3 Bion remarked once that the first scientists were grave robbers who plundered the burial grounds at the temple in Ur. This is puzzling until one realizes that the grave robbers had to defy the curse placed on them by the priests responsible for the burial ground. What distinguishes science in this view is its defiance of taboos, including the taboo against deviating from established ideas.
4 Colonus was sacred to Prometheus, who brought fire to mankind, and a suburb of Athens, the city sacred to Athena, goddess of wisdom.

Bibliography

Wilfred Bion. *Transformations: Change from Learning to Growth*. Heinemann, London, 1965. Also in *Seven Servants*, Jason Aronson, New York, 1977.
Wilfred Bion. *Second Thoughts*. William Heinemann, London, 1967.
Wilfred Bion. *A Memoir of the Future*. Karnac, London, 1990.
James Boswell. *The Life of Samuel Johnson, LLD*. George Bell and Sons, London, 1889.
Donald Meltzer and Meg Harris Williams. *The Apprehension of Beauty: The Role of Aesthetic Conflict in Development, Art and Violence*. The Clunie Press, Old Ballechin, Strath Tay, UK, 1988.

7
PSYCHOANALYSIS AND SCIENCE

Introduction

The debate over the scientific status of psychoanalysis, which began with its birth at the end of the nineteenth century, has now extended well into the twenty-first. Bion, taking an expansive view of what constituted science, wrote that all investigation is ultimately scientific. As we have seen, he designated the activity of acquiring knowledge by any means whatsoever, as well as the desire or impulse behind this activity, by the letter K for knowledge. In this broad view, there are many different kinds of activity that satisfy the notion of K, from the most mathematically formal and elegant theories of physics, to what would generally be considered purely artistic productions. However much they may differ, these activities all convey some truth about the world.

When we hear the word "science", however, our vision tends to shrink until we are left only with an image of a chemist in a white smock working in a laboratory full of glassware and complex instruments, or a physicist working in a cave in Switzerland filled with multi-billion dollar instruments for breaking atoms and analyzing the debris. This type of science—so-called hard science—produces results and theoretical predictions that are detailed, precise and highly reliable. The elegance and power of these results often blind us to the fact that they constitute only a small part of scientific activity. Even in the "hard" sciences themselves, the proportion of scientific problems that can be solved by such rigorous methods is quite small. Chemists and physicists not only do not have solutions to most problems in the chemical and physical world, they do not even know how to formulate these problems. The range of our ignorance is far vaster than the range of our knowledge.[1]

Replicability: theories in experimental science and in psychoanalysis

Scientific theories that do yield precise and elegant predictions do so only because they have been repeatedly verified by rigorously controlled experimentation that produces results amenable to statistical analysis. Statistical analysis can produce results that are highly reliable and reproducible, but the reliability of these results depends on having a large number of examples to feed into the analysis. Such experimental studies are therefore confined to phenomena that are replicable. "Replicable" means that a great number of identical examples of the phenomenon in question may be studied simultaneously. The key words here are "great number", and "identical", which means that the phenomena one may study by such rigorous methods are necessarily simple.

Once established, theories in the hard sciences have predictive power that allows them to replace direct experience in future specific instances of the phenomena to which the theories apply. For example, Bernoulli's Principle, which began as an hypothesis about the relationship between the movement of a fluid and the pressure it exerts on adjacent surfaces, has been so fully verified by controlled experiment that engineers now use it to predict very precisely how much lift a certain wing design will produce. Aircraft designers need not, therefore, construct a series of wings and test them by trial and error in order to know how to build a wing with the desired amount of lift.

In sharp contrast to disciplines that can produce these general, rigorously testable theories are disciplines that study phenomena that are too complex for such formalization, an example—perhaps an extreme example—of which is psychoanalysis. The requirement of hard science for a high degree of replicability excludes psychoanalytic studies of the human mind. We cannot replicate either ourselves or our patients.

Because psychoanalytic hypotheses cannot be confirmed by rigorous experiment, they cannot be turned into general theories that can replace direct experience in specific cases the way that the theories of the experimental sciences, such as Bernoulli's Principle, can. On the contrary, to the degree that the analyst tries to emulate the aeronautical engineer by attempting to use psychoanalytic theory in place of direct trial and error experience with his patient, he falls short of analyzing the patient.

Psychoanalysts may recognize in a patient's experience an instance of some general theory or piece of knowledge he already has—"this is splitting" (or Oedipal conflict, or denial, or reaction formation, and so on). But the analyst who merely applies theories—who fails to move himself (or be moved by his experience of the analysis) beyond what was already encompassed by his theories before his encounter with the patient—is courting analytic sterility.[2] He cannot simply assume that the clinical problem at hand represents a specific instance of a general law, and apply the general law to the specific instance, since the loss of specific, idiosyncratic detail that appeal to a general theory would entail would have a disastrous effect on the appropriateness (life-likeness) of the resulting interpretation. He can arrive at his interpretation—which is a kind of ad hoc theory about the patient—only by patiently absorbing as much as he can of the detail that is unique and specific to his clinical experience with one patient.

For this reason, the analyst must maintain a state of highly polished ignorance about what the patient presents him with, until his experience of the patient impresses something on him. An aeronautical engineer who tried to design an aeroplane in this way would be a very bad engineer, having to re-invent the aeroplane the way the Wright brothers did, by trial and error, each time. An analyst who did not proceed in this way would be a very bad analyst. The psychoanalyst, for practical purposes, must re-invent the wing each time she makes an interpretation: she must "forget" her psychoanalytic theory until the patient reminds her of it.

For problems in the study of the human mind, another kind of knowledge, less precise, and less certain, is appropriate. The "theories" that express this knowledge may hardly deserve the term "theory" at all. They are working hypotheses that are informal, highly specific and subject to immediate correction.

In light of these contrasts, one might suppose that the work of the experimental scientists and the work of the psychoanalyst could hardly be more different. But one would be wrong. Examples of this informal and temporary kind of theory abound in the experimental sciences, for example the hunches or guesses a scientist makes when exploring a new area in which he is still trying to get his bearings. (An outstanding example of this is Watson and Crick's inspired guess about the molecular structure of DNA, based on X-ray data that was in itself very far from nailing down a specific structure.) This type of theory is always a work in progress. Highly informal, on-the-fly, and ad hoc, it would not be far from the mark to call it guesswork. It is far more common in the day-to-day activities of scientists, at least when they are working creatively, than is the production of rigorous, formal theories. This fluid guessing is found not only in the work of creative scientists and psychoanalysts, but also in the work of skilled craftsmen, where it takes the form of a combination of competence and curiosity and is addressed to the solution of a unique and specific problem. This know-how or savior-faire may be less prestigious than the rigor and precision of formal science, but the skilled craftsman has his own form of knowledge that is part of Bion's "K".

Formal theories in the experimental sciences are established by the construction of controlled experiments, while the informal theories of both physical science and psychoanalysis are established by the digestion of uncontrolled experience.

The place of theory in science and psychoanalysis

Scientific theories

Both psychoanalysts and physical scientists use informal, ad hoc, disposable theories that they evaluate in a less-than-rigorous way in their everyday work. Natural scientists are always generating theories as a kind of ad hoc scaffolding, the purpose of which is to facilitate their empirical investigations by expanding the range of experience that they may explore and organize. The high-level, abstract theories that end up being canonized in the textbooks, and that form the popular conception of scientific theorizing, are relatively few and far between compared to this everyday disposable theorizing.

Physicists express their ideas in mathematical form which, because they are mathematical, appear quite formal and rigorous. However, the physicist Joe Weinberg once compared the mathematical formulas that physicists use to the temporary hand-holds that a rock climber establishes during his climb. Each hand-hold more or less dictates the position of the next hand-hold. "A record of that," Weinberg said, "is a record of a particular climb. It gives you very little of the shape of the rock" (Bird and Sherwin, 2005, pp. 169–170).

Even a "hard" scientific theory of the kind that we naïvely regard as some kind of fixed truth is in fact only a map of a specific historic attempt to grapple with reality. Each step along the way is determined to a significant degree by the one preceding it. A rock hardly ever dictates a unique route by which it may be scaled, and there are almost always multiple routes up a rock. This means that a scientific theory is, as a rule, never uniquely correct. While a theory is far from being uniquely determined by the reality it is attempting to describe, it is, like the rock-climber's sequence of hand-holds, determined in surprisingly large part by its own history.[3]

If rock climbing does not give us a unique map of the rock, or even a map of the only way to scale it, it does give us a kind of familiarity with the rock itself, a feel for it, together with a kind of know-how about rock climbing. This equips the climber to make another, probably more sophisticated attempt. The benefits of scientific exploration are a theory of the matter that has been explored, which is of provisional value, and an education about the lay of the land and about how to explore, which are of permanent (even if non-codifiable) value. To put this in another way, the theoretical edifice whose construction the scientific scaffolding serves—the theories that make it into the textbooks where they are presented as solid, fixed knowledge—is, paradoxically, of only temporary value. It is a snapshot of what the scaffolding has permitted the scientist to construct to date. What is of permanent value in science is the skill required to build scaffolding.

The practising scientist is constantly building new scaffolding and dismantling old scaffolding that has served its purpose. To the scientifically unsophisticated, the purpose of a scientific theory is to answer questions. For scientists the importance of a scientific theory consists mainly of its usefulness in posing new questions that could not even have been asked before its formulation. For the scientifically unsophisticated, science is an edifice that contains knowledge. For the practising scientist, science is a craft that allows us to get a better view of how much we don't know by allowing us to ask questions we didn't even know we had.

This working type of theorizing, trying something, discarding it, trying something else then discarding it, that in the short term produces a myriad of little, forgettable theories, but in the long term produces a feel for the lay of the land, is what psychoanalysts do as well. Freud often compared his theories to the temporary scaffolding that is erected around a building under construction—a temporary means to an end (1900, p. 159, 536, 568, 598, 610; 1905, p. 217; 1940, p. 159). He believed that it was the function of a psychoanalytic theory to render itself obsolete; that it was nothing more than a crude approximation that is useful as a way of getting things started, and that beyond a certain point, it became a hindrance.

What is true of psychoanalysis as a whole is also true of each analysis. The picture of the patient that emerges from an analysis is, like the scientist's theoretical edifice, only a snapshot, and is therefore of transient validity. Freud himself reached this conclusion in his last paper, "Analysis Terminable and Interminable" (1937). What is of lasting benefit to the patient is not the picture itself, but the capacity to go on formulating new pictures over time—a feel for the rock and some know-how about climbing rocks. This point bears emphasizing: a successful analysis leaves in its wake a feel for how to observe certain mental states.

This familiarity and know-how are of lasting value. The main benefit of an analysis for the patient is that it makes the next analysis (or self-analysis) more sophisticated than the last one and more likely to have practical benefits. Despite the vast differences between psychoanalysis and physical science in terms of the nature of their formal theories, if we look at the ad hoc, scaffold type theory-building, which I would argue is the life-blood of any scientific investigation, even in the hard sciences, the two are surprisingly alike.

Intuition in science and psychoanalysis

The fact that so much of psychoanalysis involves intuition and guess-work does not, therefore, gainsay its status as a science. Weinberg studied physics at Berkeley under J. Robert Oppenheimer. Shortly after he had arrived there to begin his studies, Oppenheimer invited him to read one of his papers in place of a previously scheduled seminar that had been cancelled—a great honor for a young graduate student. But after he had delivered his paper,

> as if to compensate for the flattery, Oppenheimer told him with a sneer that what he had presented was "kid stuff". There was, he said, a "grown-up way to do this kind of problem," and he suggested that Weinberg get onto it right away. Weinberg duly spent the next three months laboring to produce an elaborate calculation. In the end, he had to report back that he could find no trace of the empirical relationship that he had predicted from his initial and very simple-minded argument. "Now you have learned a lesson," Oppenheimer told him. "Sometimes the elaborate, the learned method, the grown-up method is not as good as the simple and childishly näive method."
>
> (Bird and Sherwin, 2005, p. 169)

Both the practising physical scientist and the practising psychoanalyst are like craftsmen using ad hoc and expendable theories to acquire a feel for the problems at hand. In this pragmatic approach, näive and intuitive theories may be of greater value than ones rigorously deduced from existing knowledge. The criterion for the value of a theory in both physical science and psychoanalysis is its usefulness in moving the investigation along, in allowing the investigator to pose hitherto unaskable questions. Most of the time, rather than enshrining knowledge in a theoretical edifice of what we know, natural scientists and psychoanalysts both use small theories, picking them up when useful and dropping them just as quickly when they have served their purpose—which is usually to show us what we don't know.

Rules and games in science and psychoanalysis

Despite these similarities, one major difference between experimental physical science and psychoanalysis remains. We have already touched on it: physical sciences have high-level general theories that psychoanalysis lacks. Does psychoanalysis have anything comparable? The answer, I believe, is yes and no. The philosopher Ludwig Wittgenstein has likened certain kinds of human activities to games. A game is defined by a set of rules. If you follow all the rules, you are playing a certain game. If you do not follow the rules, you are not playing that game. A specific scientific discipline is an example of what Wittgenstein would call a game. The rules of a science game are certain fundamental premises—notions without which a given scientific discipline would not exist. For example, the notions of space, time and mass may be regarded as fundamental premises of physics. It is difficult to imagine what physics would look like if any of those notions were discarded. Similarly, the notion of natural selection is a fundamental premise in evolutionary biology: it is difficult to imagine any theory in modern evolutionary biology that does not depend, directly or indirectly, on the validity of the notion of natural selection.

What this means is that one may reject these premises, but it is difficult to imagine then going on to do physics or evolutionary biology in any form that would be recognizable. Like the rules of a game, one may accept these premises or not, but one cannot both reject them and still play the game for which they are the rules (although one may, of course, reject them and play another game, with different rules). These rules or fundamental premises are not subject to debate within a discipline. They are, so to speak, sovereign. They set the terms of the debate within a discipline, and, like the sovereignty of nations, they limit the legitimate criticism that one discipline can make of another that has different rules or fundamental premises. These fundamental notions define a certain game, a certain discipline, and all those who accept them are playing the same game, however much their activities within the game may otherwise differ.

In sciences such as physics, biology and physical medicine, these fundamental premises may be combined with new observations to produce theories. A physicist could say, "given the ideas of space, time and mass, what happens when we move masses through space over time?" Observations have pointed to certain regularities, which have been embodied in Newton's laws of the motion of masses in space and time. Theories such as these are subsidiary to the fundamental premises in a field in the sense that they may turn out to be true or false (or only partly true, as, for example, Einstein's revision shows Newton's laws of motion to be). But even if subsidiary theories are shown to be false, the fundamental premises remain valid.

Subsidiary theories that have been verified many times in many different ways come to be regarded as well established, and eventually achieve the status of a fact within the scientific discipline. For example, the fundamental notions of space, time and mass in physics, when combined with experimental observation, yield Newton's theory of motion, a subsidiary theory that has been tested and confirmed so many times in so many different ways that it is now regarded as a kind of fact, and called a scientific law. The fundamental notion of natural selection in Darwin's theory of evolution, when combined with observation, gives rise to specific theories that are typically and characteristically part of evolutionary theory. These theories in turn give rise to certain predictions, which can then be tested against observation.

Psychoanalysis also has a set of premises that are shared by all psychoanalysts—ideas that seem to be basic rules of the psychoanalytic game. Among them are the notions of an unconscious and of psychological defense mechanisms (which are by definition unconscious). It would be difficult to imagine how a psychoanalyst would function if he did not accept these notions.

However, the resemblance between psychoanalysis and physical science stops there. Despite it, psychoanalysts, unlike physicists, biologists or physicians, have not been able to combine their fundamental notions with new observations to give rise to well established subsidiary theories. They have generated subsidiary theories, and have tested them against their clinical experience, but they have not been able to combine these observations with their fundamental premises to generate theories that, like Newton's laws, have become part of a theoretical canon.

This point may require some elaboration. Consider the germ theory of disease, which holds that certain illnesses are caused by microorganisms, that these diseases may be transmitted from one person to another by physical transmission of these organisms, that the disease in question cannot occur in the absence of these organisms, and so on. This theory is not one of the fundamental premises of medicine, since we could imagine medicine without it (as it was before the mid-nineteenth century—very different from modern medicine, but still recognizably medicine). But as a theory, it has been tested in so many and varied situations that its validity is universally accepted by physicians. It is quite a well-established theory.

With this in mind, consider any psychoanalytic theory, such as the theory of the Oedipus complex. Today, even this theory is not accepted by some analysts who still subscribe wholeheartedly to the fundamental premises of psychoanalysis (the unconscious and psychological defense). At the same time, there are other analysts who cannot imagine thinking psychoanalytically without this theory. For the former group, the Oedipus complex is a contingent phenomenon, arising only as a consequence of certain less-than-optimal childhood environments. For the latter group, it is part of the foundation of their psychoanalytic picture of the mind. Analysts in this group cannot picture psychoanalysis without it. In neither case is it a well established theory in the same way that the germ theory of disease is a well established theory in medicine: for one group it is a theory but not well established, and for the other it is well established, but not a theory (since it is for them a fundamental premise—an indispensable part of their approach to the patient).

Take, for another example, the theory of projective identification in psychoanalysis. There are many analysts who regard it as having questionable validity, and as not very useful in any event. There are others who would be hard pressed to practise analysis without it. I don't mean they would find it difficult to treat only certain patients, the way a physician would if she didn't have the germ theory. I mean they would be hard pressed to treat any patient without it. The former type of analyst regards projective identification as a more or less dispensable idea, while the latter finds it a fundamental part of their psychoanalytic concept of how the mind works, indispensable in all cases.

I could add to these examples. Others writers could certainly suggest other examples, and still others would quarrel with the ones I have chosen. But the point I am trying to make is that notions in psychoanalysis that are universally accepted tend to fall into the category of fundamental premises—ideas without which practising the discipline would be hard to imagine—and ideas that do not fall into this category tend not to be universally accepted. This is what I meant when I wrote above that psychoanalysts have not been able to generate subsidiary theories which, like those of physics or evolutionary biology, have won universal acceptance among workers in the field. In psychoanalysis, the only notions that are well established and universally accepted are fundamental premises.[4]

We must conclude that the fundamental premises of psychoanalysis do not act like foundational structures that can link with observation to generate subsidiary theories. Instead, they act like guidelines that dictate a general approach to patients. The psychoanalytic notion of the unconscious (like the Hippocratic notion of physical causation and physical treatment of disease) points to such a general approach to the patient, a certain way of listening to, observing and thinking about patients. The ideas of the unconscious and defense define the psychoanalytic approach to the patient, and distinguish it from the religious, magical or medical approaches, as well as from the approach taken by non-psychoanalytic psychologies.

Psychoanalysis does not have fundamental premises on which a hierarchical system of subsidiary theories may be built. Rather, it has in place of a rigorous theoretical system what might be called a set of conceptual tools, ideas that represent a certain way of looking at things, and that act as instruments that make certain kinds of observations possible. As the skilled craftsman has a set of tools that allows him to shape his materials in a certain way, the psychoanalyst has a set of tools that allows him to conceptualize her experiences in a certain way.

Psychoanalysis is not a theoretical structure, like Newtonian physics, only with Freud standing in for Newton. It is a practice that allows us to see certain things in a certain way, and to ask certain questions that were unaskable without it. It provides an approach to problems that we cannot even begin to formulate using the methods of physical science. In this way, psychoanalysis makes it own unique contribution to scientific knowledge.

Notes

1 As Werner Heisenberg put it, "The existing scientific concepts cover always only a very limited part of reality, and the other part that has not yet been understood is infinite. What we observe is not nature itself, but nature exposed to our method of questioning" (Heisenberg, 1958, p. 26).
2 In John Rickman's words, "no research without therapy, no therapy without research" (Rickman, 1957, p. 213).
3 For example, there are at least three different, independent methods for arriving at the physical law known as conservation of energy—three different routes, starting at three different places, that arrive at the same destination.
4 As the above examples have indicated, although certain fundamental premises, such as the notion of the unconscious and of defense mechanisms, are shared by all analysts, different groups of analysts share additional fundamental premises. Wittgenstein might say that these different fundamental premises are actually different rules of the game, and that the different groups of analysts are therefore playing different games. What this means for the status of psychoanalysis as a unitary discipline is an interesting question that I cannot go into now, except to say that it may have something to do with the historical tendency of psychoanalysis to fragment into different groups.

Bibliography

Kai Bird and Martin J. Sherwin. *American Prometheus: The Triumph and Tragedy of J. Robert Oppenheimer*. Alfred A. Knopf, New York, 2005.

Sigmund Freud. The interpretation of dreams. *The Standard Edition of the Complete Psychological Works of Sigmund Freud*, 4–5, 1900.

Sigmund Freud. Three essays on the theory of sexuality. *The Standard Edition of the Complete Psychological Works of Sigmund Freud*, 7:130–243, 1905.

Sigmund Freud. Analysis terminable and interminable. *The Standard Edition of the Complete Psychological Works of Sigmund Freud*, 23:209, 1937.

Sigmund Freud. An outline of psycho-analysis. *The Standard Edition of the Complete Psychological Works of Sigmund Freud*, 23:144–267, 1940.

Werner Heisenberg. *Physics and Philosophy*. Penguin Books, London, 1958.

John Rickman. Methodology and research in psycho-pathology. In *Selected Contributions to Psycho-analysis*. Hogarth Press and the Institute of Psycho-Analysis, London, 1957.

8
THE CRAFT OF PSYCHOANALYSIS

> ... we must conclude that education is not what it is said to be by some, who profess to put knowledge into a soul that does not possess it, as if they could put sight into blind eyes. On the contrary, our own account signifies that the soul of every man does possess the power of learning the truth and the organ to see it with; and that, just as one might have to turn the whole body round in order that the eye should see light instead of darkness, so the entire soul must be turned away from this changing world until its eye can bear to contemplate reality and that supreme splendor that we have called the Good. Hence there may well be an art whose aim would be to effect this very thing, the conversion of the soul, in the readiest way; not to put the power of sight into the soul's eye, which already has it, but to ensure that, instead of looking in the wrong direction, it is turned the way it ought to be.
> —Plato, *The Republic*, Book 7 (518c)

> ... we must do away with all explanation, and description alone must take its place. And this description gets its light, that is to say its purpose, from the philosophical problems. These are, of course, not empirical problems; they are solved rather, by looking into the workings of our language, and that in such a way as to make us recognize those workings: in despite of an urge to misunderstand them. The problems are solved, not by giving new information, but by arranging what we have always known. Philosophy is a battle against the bewitchment of our intelligence by means of language.
> —Ludwig Wittgenstein, *Philosophical Investigations*, §109

In 2001, the Swiss psychoanalyst Giovanni Vassalli published "The Birth of Psychoanalysis From the Spirit of Technique" (Vassalli, 2001). It addressed the issue of the scientific status of psychoanalysis from a unique and compelling perspective.

Vassalli points out that, although most psychoanalysts believe that psychoanalysis is a science, and that they are themselves scientists, in reality they do not behave like scientists and never have.

In science, progress is typically achieved through a kind of cycle or spiral: someone proposes an hypothesis about something, someone devises an experiment to test it, the results of the experiment then either support the hypothesis, or suggest a modified hypothesis (or an altogether different one), which someone then subjects to further experimental testing, and so on.

This means that, if psychoanalysis is indeed a kind of science, psychoanalysts should propose hypotheses about the human psyche, which they should then test by some appropriately designed controlled experiment, which would then lead to new hypotheses and experimental tests. This they never do.

Vassalli enlisted Freud's support for the view that psychoanalysis is fundamentally different from the experimental sciences:

> In 1930, the physicist Heinrich Löwy asked Freud to write a contribution to a collection of solutions to problems in science. After some effort, Freud replied that, "in trying to find some suitable examples I have encountered strange and almost insuperable obstacles." At first, he seems to have felt that these obstacles were due to a block or a resistance within himself, causing him to feel that "certain procedures that can be expected from other fields of investigation could not be applied to my subject matter" (Freud, 1961, p. 395).
>
> *(Vassalli, 2001, p. 3)*

But after further soul-searching, he concluded that this was not a block, but an insight instead, and that in fact, "within the methods of our work there is no place for the kind of experiment made by physicists and physiologists" (ibid.).

Psychoanalysis and science

Vassalli says that Freud had such difficulty coming up with a good example of a scientific solution to a psychoanalytic problem because to do so would have meant discarding some of his deep and unwavering convictions about psychoanalysis. The first of these was that "the discovery of the unconscious has swept away all previously formulated problems" (i.e. all problems in psychology as previously formulated, which now needed to be reformulated in terms of the unconscious; Vassalli, 2001, p. 4). The second was that knowledge of the unconscious can be gained only by a method of observation unlike that of experimental science.

Let us stop to consider how radical these claims are: Freud claims to have discovered something—the unconscious—whose role in the operation of the mind is so fundamental that all questions in psychology must be reformulated to take it into account, because what had theretofore been regarded as the mind was only a part of the mind—the conscious part—and that this conscious part was like a leaf floating on the surface of the unconscious. Trying to explain the activity of the conscious mind without reference to the mind's unconscious dynamics was like trying to account for the motions of the leaf floating on a stream without reference to the motions of the stream. He said furthermore that this unconscious part of the mind, so crucial to understanding anything important about the mind, was so utterly uncanny—so different from anything that science had yet considered—that it could not be investigated by any accepted scientific method.

It is hard to overestimate the boldness of these claims. Freud was saying, in effect, that he had discovered something about the mind without which one simply cannot understand anything important about it, and that only he knew the method by means of which it might properly be explored. It is easy to see why critics of psychoanalysis might feel that these claims, taken in their stark simplicity, were simply mad. Supporters of psychoanalysis have tended to respond to this criticism by becoming apologists, arguing that things are not as bad (i.e., as radical) as they seem—that psychoanalysis really is a science like other sciences, but an embryonic one whose eventual experimental validation was only a question of time. Other analysts have argued that the scientific status of psychoanalysis is moot, because it is really a form of some other discipline such as hermeneutics or linguistics. Both approaches remove psychoanalysis from the radical position in which Freud placed it.

Vassalli suggests that neither the critics of psychoanalysis nor its apologists have thought seriously enough about what Freud actually wrote, that they have treated his texts "in an unconsidered and eclectic way" (Vassalli, 2001, p. 4), and that they have not considered carefully the question of the method by means of which psychoanalytic constructs are validated in practice. He argues that this method is neither that of experimental science nor of philosophy, and says that its blueprint can be found elsewhere, in the Greek idea of *techne*, a form of investigation that was recognized in classical times, but which faded from European thought around the time of Descartes.

The origins of psychoanalysis

In his paper, Vassalli adopts an expository method of gathering disparate threads that together form a plausible but unproven picture (which is precisely the method of *techne* and the kind of result it produces). The first thread he picks up is the importance to Freud of naturalistic (non-experimental) observation of the type that is found in astronomy or population genetics. When Freud was a young researcher, medicine was being swept up in a rising tide of enthusiasm for physiological experimentation. He found Brücke's laboratory to be an island of tolerance on which the old-style non-experimental observation of microscopic anatomy was still valued. He also found in the person of Charcot a mentor whose capacity to learn through naturalistic observation was highly developed. Vassalli writes that, in his obituary of Charcot, Freud relates how he was able to utilize his "special gift" with a vast range of patients suffering from chronic nervous diseases, describing him as not a meditative thinker but rather an artistically gifted and visual mind, a seer.[1] Based on Charcot's own account, Freud gives the following description of his way of working: "He used to look again and again at things he did not understand, to deepen his impression of them day by day, till suddenly an understanding of them dawned on him. In his mind's eye the apparent chaos presented by the continual repetition of the same symptoms then gave way to order: the new nosological pictures emerged, characterized by the constant combination of certain groups of symptoms" (Freud, 1893a, p. 12).

(Vassalli, 2001, p. 5)[2]

Vassalli says that in Freud's characterization of Charcot's method, certainty

> … is not left to external verification by experiment; it arises independently from the process of visual perception … This desire was also familiar to Charcot, as Freud here emphasizes: "He might be heard to say that the greatest satisfaction a man could have was to see something new, that is, to recognize it as new" (Freud, 1893a, p. 12).
>
> *(Vassalli, 2001, p. 5)*

"New" as opposed to "already known and understood". Freud's approach to an understanding of the mind, which followed Charcot's, was to observe the patient without prejudice (i.e., while suspending judgement about the significance of what he was observing) until a picture emerged—an ad hoc theory suggested by the mass of observation itself. Theoretical preconceptions tend to be general; that is, they tend to refer to types or classes of phenomena of which the present instance is an example. By deliberately keeping his theoretical preconceptions at bay, Freud protected his capacity to see what was new or unique about this patient from what he already knew about the type of patient he was dealing with.

Scientists also employ this kind of open observation to arrive at new theoretical ideas through a kind of inspiration when they are dealing with areas about which very little is known. A well-documented example of this is Watson and Crick's inspired guess about the structure of DNA, based on data from X-ray crystallography that, however informative, was still quite far from specifying an exact structure.

But, as we saw in the previous chapter—and here is the crux of the difference between psychoanalysis and the experimental sciences—once scientists arrive at their conjectures, they frame them in the form of hypotheses and design experiments with which they may be tested. These experiments are precisely what Freud told Löwy he could find no place for in his work.

By the time he wrote An Outline of Psychoanalysis ten years after his letter to Löwy, Freud had left experiment even more explicitly to the natural sciences: "We have discovered technical methods of filling up the gaps in the phenomena of our consciousness, and we make use of those methods just as a physicist makes use of experiment" (Freud, 1940, pp. 196–197). Here "just as" means "instead of". But what are these technical methods?

At this point, Vassalli drops this thread and pick up another that he found in Freud's paper on "Psychical (or Mental) Treatment" (Freud, 1890), in which he wrote that, following the emergence of medicine from the sphere of natural philosophy into that of natural science, and the consequent astonishing advances made during the early and mid-nineteenth century in the understanding and treatment of physical disease,

> ... it followed, as a result of an incorrect although easily understandable trend of thought, that physicians came to restrict their interest to the physical side of things and were glad to leave the mental field to be dealt with by the philosophers whom they despised.
> (Vassalli, 2001, p. 6)

Freud did not in any way lack appreciation for the profound scientific revolution in physical medicine that had begun in his lifetime. But he had no taste for the trend to treat the mind as something that could be explained entirely by reference to physiologic processes (a trend that continues to this day to be the subject of fierce debate). On the contrary, Freud was quite positively interested in the possibility of treating the mind in its own right. He defined such "psychical treatment" unambiguously as follows:

> "Psyche" is a Greek word which may be translated "mind". Thus "Psychical treatment" means "mental treatment". The term might accordingly be supposed to signify "treatment of the pathological phenomena of mental life". This, however, is not its meaning. "Psychical treatment" denotes, rather, treatment taking its start in the mind, treatment (whether of mental or physical disorders) by measures which operate in the first instance and immediately upon the human mind. Foremost among such measures is the use of words; and words are the essential tool of treatment.
> (Freud, 1890, p. 283)

Freud pointed out that the ancient tradition of mental treatment (that is, treatment based on an appreciation of the influence of the mind upon the patient's physical well-being, and of the possibility of the physician's influencing the mind directly and through it the body indirectly) had languished during the period of the development of scientific physical medicine, "in spite of all the advances in the methods of investigation made by physical medicine" (1890, p. 284).[3]

To adherents of the new scientific medicine, the idea of the mind in its own right, as a subject worthy of study independent of whatever physiologic processes were related to it, appeared to be no more than a Romantic indulgence. The problem for analysts is to show that psychoanalysis is not just the last gasp of late Romanticism. But, Vassalli says, "the pressure and impatience of the time led to generations of analysts after Freud generally resolving this Gordian knot by simply cutting through it" (Vassalli, 2001, pp. 6–7).

The way in which psychoanalysts have cut through this knot is by simply declaring that psychoanalysis is a science, just like the "hard" (experimental) sciences, though perhaps still in its embryonic stages, despite the fact that the sine qua non of modern natural science, controlled experimental testing of hypotheses, was nowhere to be found in psychoanalysis.[4]

Official declarations notwithstanding, the fact remains that by postulating the existence of a hidden daemonic force that he christened the unconscious, Freud appeared to be engaging in Romantic fantasies; by claiming to be able to discern through a kind of heightened sensitivity what was unconscious in his patients, he appeared to be claiming to be able to read minds; and by claiming to be able to influence it by the use of words, he appeared to be engaging in the use of magical incantations.

It is customary for psychoanalysts to attribute the resistance that psychoanalysis has encountered from non-analysts to the fact that it has uncovered repressed psychological forces, and to dismiss objections to psychoanalysis as mere attempts at mass re-repression of what psychoanalysis has uncovered. But those who would attribute opposition to psychoanalysis solely to resistance to its concepts should consider how bizarre these claims of Freud's appear to be.

Freud's technique

How accurate are these appearances? Freud was no believer in mind-reading, as he indicated in a passage in his paper on mental treatment in which he discusses psychic mediums:

> ... what is known as "thought-reading" [*Gedanken erraten*] may be explained by small, involuntary muscular movements carried out by the "medium" in the course of an experiment—when, for instance, he has to make someone discover a hidden object [without giving any ostensible prompting]. The whole phenomenon might be more suitably described as "thought-betraying" [*Gedanken verraten*].
>
> *(Freud, 1890, p. 288)*

Vassalli says that the play on the words *verraten* (betray) and *erraten* (guess) contains a basic dynamic that Freud used in his later technique. He relies on information that the patient betrays (intentionally or not) in order to make his "guesses" about what is in the patient's mind, but unknown to him. In addition to verbal cues, such as the temporal association or sequence of ideas and observations of what might normally have been said, but was not, at a certain point in the session, this information is conveyed to the analyst through non-verbal communications such as body language, intonation and the "music" of speech. The basic technical approach of the psychoanalytic clinician relies far more heavily on information conveyed unconsciously by song-and-dance than by the mere verbal productions of the patient.

Vassalli then takes up the question of how Freud guessed. He wrote that, in *Studies on Hysteria*,

> [Freud's description of his] technique of suggestion repeatedly demonstrates how much is based on the doctor having to "more or less divine" the nature of the case and the motives for the defense that are operating in the patient. It is the recurrent mention of this guessing that describes the precise technical act that opens up access to the unconscious. When the guess is correct, resistance is removed, enabling the patient to reproduce the pathological impressions, and to articulate them in an expression of feeling. "The situation may be compared with the unlocking of a locked door, after which opening it by turning the handle offers no further difficulty" (Breuer and Freud, 1895, p. 283).
>
> (Vassalli, 2001, p. 5)

This passage may require some explanation. As we have seen, Freud's original (pre-psychoanalytic) therapeutic technique consisted of exerting psychological pressure on the patient to come up with the pathogenic, repressed memory that was supposed to underlie the patient's manifest symptoms. (This psychological pressure in the form of exhortations to remember was occasionally combined with physical pressure on the patient's forehead.) Freud observed, quite reasonably, that if he needed pressure to get the patient to remember something, then there must be some resistance within the patient blocking the memory and requiring the pressure. Eventually he realized that if he listened in a certain way to the patient, the resistance betrayed itself, enabling him to guess it and enlighten the patient about it. The repressed memory would then spring forth, and the pathogenic impressions would be released in a rush of emotion. In time, Freud's technique shifted from forcing the patient to recall despite his resistances, to guessing the resistance and allowing the patient to recall what he had repressed. Vassalli goes on:

> The guessing of a resistance, now firmly established as a technical instrument, expresses more precisely what our more familiar expression interpret [*deuten*] leaves obscure. In other words: guessing is a precise form of interpretation. In the history of the techniques it replaces for Freud the strenuous "forcing of hypnosis". He therefore begins increasingly to doubt the therapeutic use of hypnosis, while at the same time gaining valuable insights into the newly opening space of the setting (2001).
>
> (Vassalli, 2001, p. 9)

If Freud used "guessing" in this sense as one limb of his therapeutic technique, the other limb consisted of the use of words to influence the patient's mind and body, an idea that smacks of magic. He was aware of this, pointing out that "mere" words do indeed have the power to affect the mind in compelling ways. He believed that, just as there was a non-magical explanation for mind-reading, there must be a non-magical explanation for the apparently magical power of words, and he set about trying to find it. Today, we can say that both "mind reading" and "the magic of words" rest largely on the phenomena of song-and-dance.

At this point, Vassalli again drops the thread of his argument and picks up another (his third), that of the primacy for Freud of representational fidelity. He points out that, *In Studies on Hysteria*, Freud acknowledges, unapologetically, that his work lacks theoretical coherence:

> I am making use here of a number of similes, all of which have only a very limited resemblance to my subject and which, moreover, are incompatible with one another. I am aware that this is so, and I am in no danger of overestimating their value. But my purpose in using them is to throw light from different directions on a highly complicated topic which has never yet been represented. I shall therefore venture in the following pages to introduce similes in the same manner, though I know this is not free from objection.
> *(Breuer and Freud, 1895, p. 291)*

Vassalli comments that "the intention to illustrate, i.e. not to sacrifice visual meaning to anticipated abstract postulations [or logical coherence], is a particularly clear characteristic of Freud's investigations of the mind" (Vassalli, 2001, p. 10). It is Freud's intention here to shield his hunches from logical criticism while he is in the process of formulating them. The creative work permitted by use of ad-hoc, disposable scaffold-type theories is fortunately not constrained by considerations of logical rigor or consistency.

In the same vein, Freud advised those who had difficulty interpreting their dreams to pay attention to Schiller's advice about creative blocks:

> The ground for your complaint seems to me to lie in the constraint imposed by your reason upon your imagination. I will make my idea more concrete by means of a simile. It seems a bad thing and detrimental to the creative work of the mind if Reason makes too close an examination of the ideas as they come pouring in—at the very gateway, as it were. Looked at in isolation, a thought may seem very trivial or very fantastic; but it may be made important by another thought that comes after it, and, in conjunction with other thoughts that may seem equally absurd, it may turn out to form a most effective link. Reason cannot form any opinion upon all this unless it retains the thought long enough to look at it in connection with the others. On the other hand, where there is a creative mind, Reason—so it seems to me—relaxes its watch upon the gates, and the ideas rush in pell-mell, and only then does it look them through and examine them in a mass. You critics, or whatever else you may call yourselves, are ashamed or frightened of the momentary and transient extravagances which are to be found in all truly creative minds and [only] whose longer or shorter duration distinguishes the thinking artist from the dreamer. You complain of your unfruitfulness because you reject too soon and discriminate too severely.
> *(Freud, 1900, p. 135)*

Vassalli now begins to draw his threads together, suggesting that Freud's work was like that of an artist or craftsman:

> ... what is unexpected in the methodology of *The Interpretation of Dreams* is that while Freud refers to the [experimental] science that was still becoming established in his time, he also falls back on that great ancient tradition of Greek *techne*, which even in the eighteenth century was on the point of being completely forgotten and had long ceased to hold any appeal for psychiatry at the turn of the [twentieth] century. It should be stressed first of all that the *techne* taken from Freud is not what we generally understand today by technique—a practice based on a notion of perfect functional ability that corresponds to the mechanical model. According to ancient tradition it is based much more on that special use of reason that is appropriate for artistic production: poiesis ...
>
> (Vassalli, 2001, p. 13)

This new treatment of the mind also cast doubt on the procedure of holding to what was given and factual, in order to recast it by abstraction into a theory, with the aim of establishing generally valid concepts. With *The Interpretation of Dreams* psychoanalytic technique crossed a rubicon. Just as after the analysis using his technique in "Irma's injection" Freud could say with relief: "We find ourselves in the full daylight of a sudden discovery" (Freud 1900, p. 122)—namely that the dream is a wish-fulfillment—so he could state at the beginning of the seventh chapter: "We have been obliged to build our way out into the dark" (ibid., p. 549). Here reason is understood in a hunch-following, conjectural sense in order to investigate an "as yet unrepresented object of thought", unconscious representations and fantasies.

The process by means of which psychoanalytic activity proceeds is very different from the formation, testing and application of scientific hypotheses. Vassalli says that the mental process of the psychoanalyst (i.e., guessing) "is fundamentally distinct from a logic that starts out from unambiguous facts, then is developed into a theory, and finally leads to applications" (Vassalli, 2001, p. 16).

This fundamental distinction has stirred up doubts in the minds of many analysts about the legitimacy of their discipline. But instead of addressing these doubts directly, many analysts have shifted the problem

> ... to a supposedly more important question, which increasingly became identified with the survival of psychoanalysis: how could psychoanalysis free itself from it speculative vagueness and achieve validation as an exact science?
>
> Many analysts therefore began to make sustained efforts to bring their work into line with a general scientific approach, in order not to be left behind by progress as they chose to understand it. From the basis of a similar concern about Freud's legacy, other analysts who were attempting to avoid the danger of scientism borrowed some methodological aspects of philosophical

hermeneutics, an art of interpretation that brought psychoanalysis very close to the interpretation of literary texts, but remained almost entirely innocent in relation to the unconscious or simply treated it in terms of linguistic statement.
(Vassalli 2001, p. 17)

Vassalli observes wryly that,

it is questionable whether psychoanalytic technique has become either more exact and efficient in the first case or more creative in the second. It is more natural to suppose that in both these options cited here it has lost something of its specific quality. The increasingly formalized model, which was borrowed from cognitive science, and also the merging of horizons practised by hermeneuticists, are a very poor substitute for the imagining and guessing of unconscious processes. Neither did efforts to humanize the supposedly soulless mechanics of technique through greater empathy satisfy Freud as a method.
(Vassalli, 2001, p. 17)

The result of generations of psychoanalysts evading, rather than exploring, their doubts about psychoanalysis can be seen in the contrast between Freud's definition of psychoanalysis and the official definition of today. In 1923, Freud defined psychoanalysis as follows:

Psychoanalysis is the name (1) of a procedure for the investigation of mental processes which are almost inaccessible in any other way, (2) of a method (based on that investigation) for the treatment of neurotic disorders and (3) of a collection of psychological information obtained along these lines, which is gradually being accumulated into a new scientific discipline.
(Freud, 1923, p. 233)

Compare this with a recent definition of psychoanalysis formulated by a committee of the International Psychoanalytic Association:

The term "psychoanalysis" refers to a theory of personality structure and function and to a specific psychotherapeutic technique. This body of knowledge is based on and derived from the fundamental psychological discoveries made by Sigmund Freud.
(International Psychoanalytic Association, 2001, pp. 27–28, Article 3)

While in Freud's definition, the method of investigation gives rise to the method of treatment as well as to scientific theories, in the IPA definition, the theories are

made into a better guarantee of analytic science than the technique could be. But in this the principle of psychoanalysis as technique as Freud understood it is reversed and its origins are obscured.

This epistemic reversal has brought psychoanalysis since Freud into a fundamentally different position, characterized by a tendency to integrate it into the concept of a modern science without regard to the question of its appropriacy for the actual subject matter of psychoanalysis. This seems to justify the conclusion that it is no longer a question of "building out into the dark", but of the assertion of a methodological premise for which certainty and evidence are the most important criteria. The historical consequences of this adaptation are immense and a completely different light would be shed on many contemporary questions about psychoanalytic science if this background were taken into account.

(Vassalli, 2001, p. 19)

Techne

Vassalli now gives his view of the "technical methods" that Freud employed in place of scientific experimentation. He finds Freud's method to be a revival of *techne*, a term the ancient Greeks used for the process required for the practical production of a specific object. Vassalli distinguishes between *techne* and the modern notion of technique.

Technique is a term that may be applied to the activity of a dentist, or an accountant, or a surgeon. To say that a surgeon has good technique, or is a good technician, is high praise. Good surgical technique can be codified, taught and applied as a set of general operating principles good for any surgical problem. There is a one best way to perform a surgical procedure within the confines of existing knowledge and technology, and that way consists of the flawless application of good surgical technique.

Techne is a term that would describe the activity of an architect faced with a building site, a budget and a specified size and use for the proposed structure. There is no one best way to solve the problem, but only better or worse—more or less apposite, intelligent and creative—ways.

The result of the practice of *techne* is quite different from the result of the application of technique. While a surgeon may perform a very successful cancer surgery by the application of good surgical technique, he is unlikely to learn much either about cancer or surgery by doing so. But an architect has the opportunity to learn a great deal about the site on which he is building, about the architectural solutions to the specific problem that are possible on that site, and about new possibilities for applying existing building technologies to solve the problem he is facing.

Techne, unlike technique, not only provides the opportunity to learn about the problem as one tries to solve it, but requires that one learn approaches tailored to the unique and specific problem at hand. These approaches were not known beforehand, but have to be developed ad hoc. They cannot be codified for subsequent application to future problems (although they may be used in the future, after it is determined on an ad hoc basis that they are appropriate to the new problem).

Techne is, says Vassalli,

> ... thoughtful examination (theoria) of the way in which the production of a thing is carried out. This thoughtful observation is not abstract speculation; it accompanies the concrete process of production in the sense of a kind of savoir-faire ... [It] ... takes effect only in skillful activity and is contained in this. Such a technique is therefore an actual instrument of investigation and discovery ... when something is produced [by *techne*] the resulting work ... can be understood only as it emerges".
>
> *(Vassalli, 2001, p. 19)*

While the subject matter appropriate to scientific theory is the mechanical world of physics or physiology, the subject matter appropriate to *techne* is the animate world of the mind.

In the ancient Greek view,

> in the area between science [where certain knowledge is possible] and chance [where no knowledge is possible] essential human activities develop along with their 'subjects', for which in Aristotle a particular form of skillful knowledge is appropriate. It is that of ethics and of the arts, especially the arts of healing and rhetoric. These arts (technai) develop on the basis of a characteristic and specific rationality.
>
> *(Vassalli, 2001, p. 19)*

A "characteristic and specific rationality" means an idiosyncratic logical structure: each product of these arts evolves through a unique process of reasoning (understood as a site-specific working out of the appropriate means of accomplishing the task at hand) and their own *raison d'être*. Vassalli goes on, "it is on this kind of use of reasoning that technique as understood by Aristotle is based. To the Greeks its kinship with chance [i.e., its inherent uncertainty] was no reason to devalue it" (Vassalli, 2001, p. 19).

Vassalli comments that Freud's

> ... description of technical work [resembles *techne* in that] the subsequent theories [i.e., theories developed ad hoc during the investigation] should not be "made" in advance; "they must fall into one's house as uninvited guests while one is occupied with the investigation of details" (Freud to Ferenczi in August 1915, (Grubrich-Simitis, 1987, p. 83).
>
> *(Vassalli, 2001, p. 22)*

Investigation of "emergent" phenomena yields knowledge that does not have the kind of certainty that we associate with well-established scientific theories, but is rather "a hunch-based knowledge, for which a conjectural use of reason is appropriate. *Techne*, even when it is guided by an idea (*eidos*), cannot determine with certainty the success of a piece of work" (Vassalli, 2001, p. 19).

In many ways, an analyst working with a patient is like an artist exploring the aesthetic potential of a new medium. But there is a crucial difference: whereas an artist must mould his material into a shape that expresses a vision that is central to the production of the work of art, the analyst's "vision" for the patient is an entirely subordinate and dispensable part of the analysis. The analyst's interpretations are far less important than the patient's response to them. The artist is trying to produce something by moulding his material. The analyst is only trying to understand the nature of his material (the patient's mind), and he does so by doing something to it (making an interpretation) and then observing the response. An interpretation is less an attempt to mould the patient than a device for sounding his depths.

Although it may resemble the work of the artist more than that of the experimental scientist in many ways, psychoanalytic exploration is nonetheless an empirical investigation of the nature of the patient, in fact precisely the type of empirical investigation appropriate to the live, idiosyncratic world of the specific mind of a specific individual.

Notes

1 "Er war kein Grübler, kein Denker, sondern eine künstlerisch begabte Natur, wie er es selbst nannte, ein visuel, ein Seher [He was no brooder, no thinker, but an artistically gifted nature, or as he himself put it, a visuel, a seer]" (Freud, 1893b, p. 22).
2 Compare this to Bion's exposition of Poincaré's selected fact unifying a constant conjunction of otherwise disparate sensations.
3 In spite of, or because of?
4 While some psychoanalytic theories have been subjected to formal experimental proof, the results of these investigations have in general not proven relevant to the day-to-day work of psychoanalysts in anywhere near the same way that the experimental investigation of a new drug, or a new putative cause for gastric ulcer has proven relevant to the day-to-day work of physicians.

Bibliography

International Psychoanalytic Association, *Membership Handbook*, International Psychoanalytic Association, 2001.

Joseph Breuer and Sigmund Freud. Studies on hysteria. *The Standard Edition of the Complete Psychological Works of Sigmund Freud*, 2, 1895.

Sigmund Freud. Psychical (or mental) treatment. The *Standard Edition of the Complete Psycho-logical Works of Sigmund Freud*, 7, 1890.

Sigmund Freud. Charcot. *The Standard Edition of the Complete Psychological Works of Sigmund Freud*, 3:11, 1893a.

Sigmund Freud. The interpretation of dreams. *The Standard Edition of the Complete Psychological Works of Sigmund Freud*, 4–5, 1900.

Sigmund Freud. Two encyclopedia articles. *The Standard Edition of the Complete Psychological Works of Sigmund Freud*, 18, 1923.

Sigmund Freud. An outline of psycho-analysis. *The Standard Edition of the Complete Psychological Works of Sigmund Freud*, 23:144–267, 1940.

Sigmund Freud. Charcot. In *Gesammelte werke, Volume I*, 21–35. Imago Publishing Company, London, 1991, 1893b.

Sigmund Freud. *Letters of Sigmund Freud, 1879–1939*. Hogarth Press, London, 1961.

I. Grubrich-Simitis. *A Phylogenetic Fantasy: Overview of the Transference Neuroses*. Harvard University Press, Cambridge, MA, 1987.

Giovanni Vassalli. The birth of psychoanalysis from the spirit of technique. *The International Journal of Psycho-Analysis*, 82:3–25, 2001.

9
PSYCHOANALYSIS AND PLAY

While it is, of course, possible for a psychoanalyst to practise psychoanalysis without engaging in suggestion deliberately, the fundamental mechanism of suggestion—the direct synchronization of emotion through song-and-dance—is so pervasive in human interactions that it is impossible to practise psychoanalysis without engaging in suggestion unintentionally and automatically.

We engage each other constantly on a kinaesthetic, emotional and aesthetic level without knowing we are doing so. Our human tendency to dance together mentally means that we have a built-in bias towards synchronization, towards being in relationships with each other that "share embodied space of music and dance", as Malloch and Trevarthen put it, in which the "disagreements of verbal discussion" (which include critical thinking) do not weigh heavily. But critical thought is precisely what must be brought to bear on what we experience from and of others on this deep aesthetic level if our relationships are to be anything other than groupish mutual suggestion. And here is the heart of the matter: we must be sensitive in the aesthetic sense of the word to the emotional states conveyed to us by others if we are to understand anything important about them. But if we are to have minds that we can truly call our own, and not simply something that is the sum of all the aesthetic forces impinging on them, we must be able to think about our aesthetic experiences.

David Hume wrote that "reason is, and ought only to be the slave of the passions, and can never pretend to any other office than to serve and obey them" (1978, p. 415). Only through our emotional experiences and desires—what Hume called passions—are we able to be in contact with what things mean to us in a human sense, and if reason does not operate on what things mean—ultimately our passions or aesthetic experiences—it can have no humanly relevant function. It becomes sterile ratiocination. Psychoanalysis is an attempt to think about our aesthetic experiences so we may be better able to think critically about what we mean as humans.[1]

Psychoanalysis is a relationship between two people the main purpose of which—the only purpose of which, one might argue—is to study its own unfolding on the level of deep feeling. Both patient and analyst are buffeted by the unseen forces of the unconscious, like leaves floating on the surface of a rapidly flowing stream.[2] If the leaves can observe their own movement, they will learn something about the invisible currents that move them. Prominent among these invisible currents is the force of suggestion, based on the desire to control and shape the minds of others. Psychoanalysis does not and cannot avoid suggestion (it would be dead or inhuman if it did), but it does turn its focus towards suggestion that occurs inevitably and spontaneously, and thence to the forces and processes that drive it, giving us at least a chance to discover what moves us, and especially what moves us to move others, which is an important part of what we mean as humans.

Bion observed that "the progress of psycho-analysis has led to a departure from the state of affairs in which ideas of 'treatment', 'cure', and 'results' had any meaning". Moving beyond the "practical" activity of fixing psychological problems, psychoanalysis has become an exploration of the elements of mental life, providing the patient an opportunity to experience of the nature of his mind and inner world. It provides one with an experience of a world that one might have had, but probably would not have had, on his own. One of the ways it does this is by providing him with an opportunity to play with his experience of the world, free of the need to achieve something "therapeutic".

I am using the term "play" in its most serious sense. When a child plays, he learns about the external world by deploying his theories about the world in an experimental way. In his biography of the physicist Richard Feynman, James Gleick captured this aspect of playing when he wrote that,

> children are innate scientists, probing, puttering, experimenting with the possible and impossible in a confused local universe. Children and scientists share an outlook on life. If I do this, what will happen? is both the motto of the child at play and the refrain of the scientist. Every child is observer, analyst, and taxonomist constructing theories and promptly shedding them when they no longer fit. The unfamiliar and the strange—these are the domain of all children and scientists.
>
> *(Gleick, 1992, p. 19)*

The roots of experimental investigation of the world—both the everyday and more formal scientific varieties—lie in the play of infants and children. Scientists often refer to their work as "playing" with ideas or with new tools. One of the things that children explore in their play are the minds of others. Recall from Tronick's still-face experiment and from countless less formal observations of infants how they actively recruit their mothers into rapport by evoking emotional responses in them.

Children, even very young children, do not just observe other people in a passive way, sitting back and cataloguing their observations like little Baconians until a pattern emerges. They actively probe them to see what will happen—what the people they are playing with (and on) will do. Children are from an early age psychological experimentalists *avant le lettre*. One probe they use in their explorations of other minds is song-and-dance—the ability to evoke certain states of mind in another person through verbal and non-verbal behaviour.

In analysis, the patient engages in this investigative play by evoking responses in the analyst's mind. Like the child in Gleick's example, he says, "if I do this to him, what will happen?" We evoke states of mind in others for many reasons, but among these is the need to find out about their minds: one may establish contact with the part of external reality that we call other minds through a kind of psychological probing, actively provoking responses from them to see what they're made of. This kind of probing is the only way of learning anything about what people are like inside—which is what really concerns us about them anyway. A person is a mystery to us until we see how he reacts to something.

When children play, they are not just testing the world to see what it is like, they are also externalizing parts of their internal worlds. I say "externalizing" rather than "representing" because this type of play is a way of getting something from inside to outside so we can see what it is, in the spirit of E. M. Forster's question, "How do I know what I think until I've had a chance to hear what I have to say?"

Patients in analysis may evoke aspects of their internal worlds in the analyst partly so that they may explore the nature of whatever aspect of their internal reality they have evoked. The question they pose is "If I do this to the analyst, what will happen?", but more precisely it is, "If I make him feel what is inside me, what will he do?" Will he explode (i.e., is what I am evoking explosive?). Will he find it pleasurable, annoying, incomprehensible (i.e. is what I am evoking pleasurable, annoying or incomprehensible)? The analyst's response to the patient's evocation tells the patient about the probe—his own projection, a piece of his internal world.

This kind of testing allows us to learn about our internal and external realities at the same time: we learn about the minds of others by projecting into them our inner states (to see how they react), and we learn about our own inner states by using the minds of others as instruments for measuring them (by seeing how they reacted).

Here is an example of serious play:

With a great deal of self-hatred, a patient berates herself for not being tolerant enough of her husband, who was at the time being rather cold and unresponsive to her. She says that if only she would be more patient with him, his emotional needs would be satisfied, and he would in turn be able to nurture her emotionally. She seems to feel that she is merely being weak, and just needs to summon the will to pull her socks up, but in fact, it is hard not to notice when listening to her that she is at the end of her rope emotionally, struggling not to be overcome with depression. Breaking through her self-reproaches from time to time is a deep anger and resentment at her husband. When I comment on this, she pours out hatred and contempt for him. He is a weeny and a wimp. She can't stand men who are wimps.

Her contempt was striking. There was little evident sadness at her sad predicament, only hatred for wimps—herself and him. She expressed this sentiment with such force and absoluteness that I found myself unable to establish any distance from it. I felt I either had to agree with her tough assessment or join the company of wimps and become another target of it. I thought of a song called "Kill the Poor" satirizing the government's anti-poverty program. I felt like I was supposed to be discussing a problem with someone who was not only advocated that method of solving it, but couldn't imagine any other. Nor, at the moment, could I.

An interpretation began to form in my mind about her being one of the poor in the song whose existence is treated as an embarrassment, but I was very unsure how to phrase it—not to myself, but to her. I felt that any interpretation I made would lack all conviction in the face of her passionate intensity, and worse, it would only make me look soft and wimpy myself and probably get me included in her list of targets. I felt that nothing constructive could be accomplished by this, but I took a deep breath nonetheless and said, expecting a rain of sneering contempt at my cliché, that she was feeling like a baby that wasn't being properly held.

Instead of attacking, she stopped talking and appeared stunned as the session ended.

The next day, she said that, following my interpretation, her state of mind had altered for the first time in a week. The conviction that she would have to leave her husband because the marriage was hopeless (and, by thinly veiled implication, that she would have to leave her equally hopeless analysis) that had gripped her for the entire week, had suddenly lifted. She said with some embarrassment that a new film she had mentioned disliking the day before, but only in passing and without saying any more about it, had made her uncomfortable because of a scene in which the protagonist, a busy career woman who inherits a baby and feels stuck with it, was carrying the baby on her hip in a very precarious way. My patient couldn't help thinking that this was a real baby that might have been dropped for the sake of making a dramatic comment about a character in the film. Though it humiliated her to say so, my words "baby not held" the day before had produced an alteration in her whole state of mind.

What had I done? In one sense, nothing much. And that is the point. I had patiently suffered the psychological state she had evoked in me—the feeling of being a wimp analyst, a helpless baby, with no way out and no way in, impotent in the face of her "kill the poor" state of mind. This contempt was the same as that she felt for herself when she was in contact with what she regarded as her babyishness, and towards her husband for his. It was what prevented her from being able to face her babyishness, or to do anything more than perch it precariously on her hip, as though she were too important to be bothered with such things, and was stuck with it only because it had been foisted on her by a cruel fate. "Stuck with her" would not be a bad description of how I had felt at that point, too. I had resisted the temptation to do something to her—to fix her, or cure her of this hate-filled, imperiously intolerant state of mind (and at the same time, not incidentally, relieve myself of the burden of having to deal with it).

When she was creating the helpless, frustrated state of mind in me, she was, of course, practising a kind of suggestion, using verbal and non-verbal means to define my role in the relationship whether I liked it or not. She was using me as a plaything, but for very serious play. I did nothing other than allow her to use me for her purposes and then use what I could learn from my status as a plaything to talk to her about what she was doing. My restraint here was important, because any attempt to evade my assigned role, or to do something to change or "fix" her state of mind, would have meant to her that I couldn't stand the feelings she was evoking in me. And that would have only reinforced her feeling that my helplessness (or rather her helplessness, now mine by proxy) was unbearable.

Whatever I said to her, it should not have been in the form of a counter-suggestion. It should not have been the enactment of a desire to make her feel a certain way—through reassurance, threats, seduction, or anything else. Only then was there a hope that she could have taken what I said as something to think about, rather than as my having rejected the state of mind she was evoking in me by trying to cure her of it as she had done with the same state of mind in herself. If I had tried to reason with her, or pseudo-interpret what she was feeling while at the same time making her feel it was somehow wrong or ill or that she shouldn't be feeling it, or that there was a "better" way to go, she would have quite rightly taken what I said as a sign of panic in the face of what she was feeling and making me feel.

The analyst plays a part in the patient's play; not a part of his own choosing, but of the patient's choosing. The analyst must suffer his assigned role and he must restrict himself to reflecting it without trying to alter his assignment (that is, alter what the patient is evoking in him). In short, he must allow the patient to play with him without playing on the patient. He cannot be the author of the patient's mental states, he can only be their trustee. He cannot, in other words, be the type of psychotherapist that the psychoanalyst Thomas Main referred to when he wrote, "the sufferer who frustrates a keen therapist by failing to improve is always in danger of meeting primitive human behaviour disguised as treatment."

This restraint was a sign of respect for the patient. When Rosencrantz and Guildenstern, at the behest of Claudius, try to extract some information from Hamlet, he hands them a flute and insists that they play it. When they protest again and again that they do not know how, he says,

> Why, look you now, how unworthy a thing you make of me! You would play upon me, you would seem to know my stops, you would pluck out the heart of my mystery, you would sound me from my lowest note to the top of my compass; and there is much music, excellent voice in this little organ, yet cannot you make it speak? 'Sblood, do you think I am easier to be played on than a pipe? Call me what instrument you will, though you can fret me, you cannot play upon me.

The analyst's job is simply to observe the patient's inner experiences. The rest is up to the patient. The patient discovers his inner world—the parts he is unable to connect with—in the analyst through his play. Or rather, he misdiscovers them in the analyst as a step towards discovering their true origin in his internal world. This misdiscovery is the patient's best hope. Direct contact with his inner world has become impossible for various reasons (which is why the patient needs the analysis), so contact with it in an externalized form is the best he can do. The analyst allows himself to be a pawn in the patient's game so he can find out what kind of game the patient is playing, as a step towards helping the patient himself find out what kind of game he's playing. The analyst can do this only if he gives up any attempt to game the patient.

Notes

1 Hume's argument was an ethical one: that only passion has an ethical or moral dimension, that reason is ethically and morally neutral, and therefore reason can lead us to ethical conclusions only by being subservient to passion.
2 The most articulate exponent of this view was Georg Groddeck, who expressed it in "The Book of the Id" (Groddeck, 1949).

Bibliography

James Gleick. *Genius; the Life and Science of Richard Feynman*. Pantheon Books, New York, 1992.
George Groddeck. *The Book of the It*. Vintage Books, London, 1949.
David Hume. *A Treatise on Human Nature (1740)*. Clarendon, Oxford, 1978.

10
CONTAINMENT, SELF-CONTAINMENT AND IDENTIFICATION

Introduction

Bion's theory of psychoanalytic containment has taken its place alongside James Strachey's classic paper on the mutative interpretation as a general theory of how interpretation works. This chapter is an exploration of Bion's theory with an eye towards asking not only how interpretation works, but how interpretation can lead to the eventual termination of analysis, which I believe is made possible by acquiring an adequate capacity for self-containment.

The theory of the container relies on two elements known to psychoanalysts for many years prior to his work, projection and introjection, and introduces a third element, detoxification, that is unique to Bion's theory. I will briefly take up the two familiar elements before turning to detoxification.

Projection and introjection are the main building blocks of Melanie Klein's theory of an internal world built up over time through continuous, two-way interaction with the external world. Bion's theory of the container evolved from Klein's theory of the internal world.

In "Mourning and Its Relation to Manic-Depressive States", Klein postulated that,

> the baby, having incorporated his parents, feels them to be live people inside his body in the concrete way in which deep unconscious fantasies are experienced—they are, in his mind, "internal" or "inner" objects, as I have termed them. Thus an inner world is being built up in the child's unconscious mind, corresponding to his actual experiences and the impression he gains from people and the external world, and yet altered by his own phantasies and impulses … in the baby's mind, the "internal" mother is bound up with the "external" one, of whom she is a "double", though one which at once

undergoes alterations in his mind through the very process of internalization; that is to say, his image is influenced by his phantasies, and by internal stimuli and internal experiences of all kinds. When external situations which he lives through become internalized—and I hold that they do, from the earliest days onwards—they follow the same pattern: they also become "doubles" of real situations, and are again altered for the same reasons.

(Klein, 1940, p. 127)

The alteration that the external mother undergoes in the process of internalization is the consequence of projection, which operates simultaneously and in parallel with introjection. Klein called this complex process "the balance of projection and introjection". She later incorporated it into her theory projective identification. It allows the infant to establish a fluid, open line of communication between the external world and his unconscious internal world, which is influenced by the external world, but is by no means an exact copy of it.

Klein emphasized the importance of the internal world for one's mental stability (or the opposite) in "The Mutual Influences in the Development of Ego and Id", where she wrote:

The specific system of phantasies centering on the internal world is of supreme importance for the development of the ego. The internalized objects are felt by the young infant to have a life of their own, harmonizing or conflicting with each other and with the ego, according to the infant's emotions and experiences. When the infant feels he contains good objects, he experiences trust, confidence, and security. When he feels he contains bad objects, he experiences persecution and suspicion.

(Klein, 1952, p. 52)

She had emphasized the crucial role played by the infant's external world in its psychological development almost 20 years before when she wrote,

The object-world of the child in the first two or three months of its life could be described as consisting of hostile and persecuting, or else of gratifying parts and portions of the real world. Before long the child perceives more and more of the whole person of the mother, and this more realistic perception extends to the whole world beyond the mother. The fact that a good relation to its mother and to the external world helps the baby to overcome its early paranoid anxieties throws a new light on the importance of its earliest experiences. From its inception analysis has always laid stress on the importance of the child's early experiences, but it seems to me that only since we know more about the nature and contents of its early anxieties, and the continuous interplay between its actual experiences and its phantasy-life, can we fully understand why the external factor is so important.

(Klein, 1935, p. 170)

Klein's infant who feels he contains bad objects and experiences persecution and suspicion is a close relative, if not an identical twin, of Bion's infant who, experiencing an unbearable state of mind, needs a mother to provide containment for it. And Klein's infant who relies on favourable external realities to help him manage the paranoid anxieties arising in his internal world is also quite close to Bion's infant who relies on the maternal container to help him manage his own mind.

This does not, of course, mean that Bion's theory of the container is no more than warmed-over Klein. The element in his theory that is not found in Klein, the container's detoxification of what is projected in to it, is highly original.

Detoxification

The most common expression of the theory of the container is what is known as the maternal model. Bion distinguished models from theories in the following way: a theory is a general or abstract statement, whose very generality and abstraction makes it difficult to comprehend and use in practice. A model is a concrete and tangible example of the theory. Its concreteness and specificity makes it easier to grasp and apply that a theory, but the price to be paid for this is a limitation in scope. A model points to only certain aspects of the theory, ignoring those that cannot fit within its confines.

I would like to examine detoxification first from the point of view of the maternal model of containment, and then from the point of view of the broader theory of containment. In the maternal model of containment, an infant (standing for the patient) projects some unbearable anxiety or pain into the mind of its mother (standing for the analyst), who adopts a certain kind of open, receptive attitude that Bion calls reverie, and, using her capacity to think, understands what the infant cannot understand, or even think about, and returns it to the infant in a form that the infant/patient may begin to think about instead of simply evacuating. The analyst conveys the product of his reverie to the patient in the form of an interpretation that explains to the patient what he had been unable to bear, while simultaneously providing relief for the patient.

Now consider the theory. Bion's formulation of the theory of the container began in his work in the 1950s and early 1960s with psychotic patients who exhibited thought disorders. His method of investigation was psychoanalysis, and he made no modification in the technique he used with less severely ill patients to accommodate the psychosis—he just analysed it as best he could.[1] In the course of these investigations, he found that being psychoanalyzed seemed to help these psychotic patients think. This came as something of a surprise to him, since, while he had a general idea that analysis might do these patients some good, he had no specific therapeutic expectations; he was simply analysing what everyone regarded as hopeless cases to see what would happen. To account for this improvement in their condition, he devised his theory of the psychoanalytic container. The theory of the container was to begin with only an attempt to explain how psychoanalysis helps psychotic patients think.[2]

The maternal model of containment contains two ideas that are absent in Bion's theory of thinking and of psychoanalytic containment. These two additional ideas restrict the scope of the model compared to that of the theory. One of them is that containment provides understanding and the other is that it provides relief. Both of these ideas limit our view of psychoanalytic containment. In the psychoanalytic theory of the container, the container's function is only to help the patient think about something, not necessarily to provide understanding or relief. Thinking does not imply understanding, and there is no guarantee that an interpretation issuing from a properly functioning analytic container will provide relief or comfort. Psychoanalysis helps one to think, but that doesn't mean that, once thought about, one's thoughts will be a relief or even comprehensible.

It might be objected that, if psychoanalysis does not necessarily provide either relief or understanding, how can it be considered helpful? Bion's answer to this was both precise and restricted: to the question of whether it is the analyst's function to help the patient, he gave this reply:

> we are trying to say: "I will help you to know yourself … I am trying to be a mirror to reflect back to you who you are, so that you can see in what I say to you an image of your self."
>
> *(Bion, 1994, p. 219)*

With this in mind, I would like to propose a second model of containment, not to replace the maternal model, but to place alongside it. This second model, together with the maternal one, addresses certain elements that are not expressed in the maternal model, and, together with it, produces a combined model that approximates more closely to the full scope of Bion's theory of the container than does the maternal model alone. To introduce it, I'll begin with a story that may at first appear to have nothing to do with psychoanalysis.

Bion was a tank commander in the First World War, a nineteen-year-old second lieutenant whose job it was to walk in front of his tank, exposing himself to direct enemy fire while guiding the driver who was unable to see what was around him. If the tank commander was hit and fell, there was a good chance he would be run over and crushed by his own tank.

Bion was awarded the DSO, Britain's second highest military decoration, as well as the Knight's Cross of the French Legion of Honour, for his actions in the Battle of Cambrai. His citation reads as follows:

> For conspicuous gallantry, and devotion to duty. When in command of his tank in an attack he engaged a large number of enemy machine guns in strong positions, thus assisting the infantry to advance. When his tank was put out of action by a direct hit he occupied a section of trench with his men and machine guns and opened fire on the enemy. He moved about in the open,

giving directions to other tanks when they arrived, and at one period fired a Lewis gun with great effect from the top of his tank. He also got a captured machine gun into action against the enemy, and when reinforcements arrived he took command of a company of infantry whose commander was killed. He showed magnificent courage and initiative in a most difficult situation.[3]

Bion received his decoration because he was able to go about his job despite being in a situation in which he, like any sane person, would have had to have been totally terrified. But being terrified is not the same as being panicked. I tell this story to suggest that the detoxifying element of analytic containment is the ability to be in the presence of the emotional dangers that the analyst deliberately exposes herself to by being a psychoanalyst, without panicking. This kind of equanimity—what we might call grace under fire—is a pre-requisite for the ability to think.

As I mentioned earlier, Bion's theory of the container derived from his attempts to analyse psychotic patients without conceding to pressure to give reassurance, advice, direction, or to circumvent difficult issues. This approach exposed him directly to severe emotional turmoil (I mean his, not just the patient's), in the midst of which he had to keep his wits about him without losing contact with either the patient's suffering, his own suffering, or common-sense reality. The patients he analyzed posed a constant threat of acting out in the form of suicide, lawsuits and involvement of the police, and of acting in, in the form of creating in the analyst painful emotional quandaries, confusions and dilemmas. As Bion recounted repeatedly in his notebooks, the effect of this barrage was most often to reduce the analyst to a state of mental paralysis—a combination of an inability to think and a paralysing fear of the consequences of pursuing unalloyed psychoanalysis with such ill patients. The pressure to run from this situation must have been enormous, and had to be resisted.

Why bother? Why expose oneself to the danger of attempting psychoanalysis with psychotic patients (or for that matter with the psychotic part of non-psychotic patients)? The reason is that we can't avoid it. We don't get to pick and choose who our patients are going to turn out to be. We do choose them by performing an initial evaluation, but how often do our patients turn out to be more ill than we thought? And what do we do then? A thoroughgoing analysis of even a neurotic patient, if it penetrates deeply enough, will reveal an underlying unconscious psychosis. Bion believed that facing this challenge directly was the only way he could work with scientific integrity, and the only way he could responsibly deal with the patient as he or she was.

The maternal model of containment adds elements such as providing understanding and relief that are absent in the theory of containment. What the maternal model misses is as important as what it adventitiously adds: the containing analyst must be prepared to deal with destructive attacks, coming from a psychotic part of the patient, on his ability to think and to remain reasonably calm. Withstanding these attacks is what allows the analyst to think about—that is, contain—what the patient is unable contain.

It might be objected that my emphasis on the difficulty of psychoanalysing psychotic patients, while perhaps interesting in a purely historical sense, has little relevance to the problem of containment in the psychoanalysis of non-psychotic patients. I don't think Bion would have been persuaded by this objection, the cogency of which rests on one's perspective about the relationship between psychotic and non-psychotic processes. If one believes that patients are either neurotic or psychotic, then the objection carries real weight. If, on the other hand, one believes with most Kleinians that a neurosis is the product of an unconscious psychosis, then one will conclude that the analyst of even neurotic patients will have to withstand attacks on his ability to think (which are part of what Bion called attacks on linking).

To summarize, the maternal model of the theory of the container emphasizes the analyst's receptivity to the patient's projections and her capacity for reverie as an agent in the detoxification of the received projections. The model I am proposing alongside the maternal model (which might be called the paternal model of containment) emphasizes the capacity of the analyst to defend his link-forming reverie against attacks on linking emanating from the unconscious, psychotic parts of the patient's personality. The two must act in concert, as a kind of combined parental couple, for successful detoxification to occur. In addition, the presence of a paternal element in the act of containing guarantees that, like Lacan's *nom du pére*, the container-analyst's interpretation is as likely to present the patient with a developmental challenge as it is to present him with comfort or relief. The most likely impact on a well-received good interpretation would be a combination of the two: relief alongside disquiet.

Containment, self-containment and identification

As difficult as successful containment is, it is only half the battle. The patient must still sooner or later develop the capacity to do for himself what the containing analyst does for him if he is to have a successful termination to his analysis. This is self-containment. Containment by an analyst corresponds to what Melanie Klein would have called a favourable environment for the infant. A favourable environment, as she said and as we all know, is an important factor in psychological development. But it is still just an external factor. Psychological maturity and independence—self-containment—depends on developments in the internal world.

We often assume that the capacity to contain oneself eventually follows more or less automatically from the experience of being repeatedly contained, but it is not clear how this is supposed to happen. It is not obvious how being contained —having the experience of someone else who remains calm when subjected to experiences that one finds unbearable—could by itself lead to self-containment, any more than it is clear how watching a highly disciplined and talented dancer or athlete can make one a dancer or an athlete.

The answer usually given to this puzzle is that the infant (or patient) develops the capacity for self-containment through identification with the container. The term identification, along with the related terms incorporation and introjection, has a chequered history in the psychoanalytic literature. Various authors have used them in various ways, and I do not propose to discuss here the complex relationships between these ideas. Kleinians believe that the psychological process called identification rests on an unconscious fantasy of physically incorporating an object into one's body, leading to the state that we call identification. What I wish to emphasize here is not the mechanism or fantasy of incorporation per se, but rather the spirit in which the incorporation/identification occurs.

For example, identification with an object may occur as a defence against painful feelings of envy and smallness. In this case, the spirit animating the identification is hatred of envy and smallness. This type of identification is a part-object identification, since the gap or difference between self and object is denied. It produces a sense of being something one is not, an altered sense of "who I am", and provides whatever fugitive comfort may be offered by a delusion.

This type of identification seems to be present from very early in life, as Freud recognized in the final days of his life, when he wrote,

> "Having" and "being" in children. Children like expressing an object-relation by an identification: "I am the object." "Having" is the later of the two; after loss of the object it relapses into "being". Example: the breast. "The breast is a part of me, I am the breast." Only later: "I have it"—that is, "I am not it" …
>
> (Freud, 1939, p. 300)

There is a second type of identification that seems not to be defensive. Since in this form of identification, the difference between self and object is not denied, we call this identification with a whole object. As in the case of defensive, difference-denying identification, the object is "taken in", but the spirit in which this occurs is not one of hatred, envy and defensiveness, but love and gratitude. The object is taken into one's heart in the sense that one loves the object and aspires to be like it, without feeling that one *is* it. This type of identification does not lead to a delusion about who one is, but instead to psychological growth. If the container is identified with in this spirit, the result is self-containment.

This type of identification does not affect one's sense of identity in the same way as defensive identification does, since it is only a relationship with an object recognized as an object, separate from the self, which itself remains unchanged. Upon further reflection, we can see that there is even a question whether this should be regarded as a form of identification at all, since the crucial point is not an alteration of one's sense of identity, but the fact that only recognizing a container as non-self (that is, not identifying with it) and loving it as something non-self leads to self-containment. In this case, it is not simply the repeated experience of the container's ability to contain—the mother's love for the infant, in the maternal model—that leads to self-containment. It is the infant's love for the mother.

There is an ironic paradox at play here. If the container is identified with in a spirit of hatred and envy, then dependence on the hated object will be perpetuated. True independence from the container—self-containment—is the product of a relationship, based on love and gratitude, with a separate object, which implies the recognition of difference. John Steiner, in his book *On Seeing and Being Seen* (2011), touched on this point when he wrote,

> Containment [here Steiner seems to have maternal containment in mind] relieves anxiety and makes the patient feel understood, but in itself it does not allow a true separateness to be achieved ... At this stage the loss of the object during actual separations is denied by a phantasy of omnipotent possession [i.e., through defensive identification with the container/analyst]. Relief from anxiety comes from a sense of being understood by the analyst, and it relies on the analyst's authority. However, understanding has to arise from within. It depends on a capacity to think and judge for oneself, and to achieve it the patient must give up his dependence on the views and judgments of authority figures, including the analyst.
>
> Relinquishing this dependence ushers in.... a move towards independence and towards facing the pain of the mourning process. In this phase the reality of dependence on the object must first be acknowledged and the reality of the loss of the object must then be faced in order that mourning is worked through. Both are often vehemently resisted.
>
> *(Steiner, 2011, p. 16)*

I would add to Steiner's formulation the observation that acknowledgment of dependence on the object requires not just acknowledgment of dependence, but also, and prior to that, an acknowledgment of the object as whole object—meaning a person separate from the self. This acknowledgement of separateness is the loss that Steiner says must be mourned.

Clinical illustration

On the night before his initial consultation with me, a patient had the following dream. He arrived at my office for his consultation, only to find the waiting room full of people. I was nowhere in sight. He went into the consulting room, and discovered me showing another crowd of admiring people some fabrics I had designed. He felt obliged to admire them as well, but at the same time felt cheated out of his consultation. I was evidently so much in need of his praise for my work, however, that he couldn't complain.

Among his associations were the feelings that he had to serve other people, which he resented but could not complain to them about; that he felt he was never doing enough for them; and that he somehow was inadvertently always messing this obligation up. I said that the dream suggested that, although he hoped to get some help from me, he feared he would end up instead having to help me in some way. He agreed that he had dreamt of me as one more in the endless line of people who demanded his help when he needed help from them.

He was surprised and embarrassed at this portrayal of me, and added, by way of explanation and apology, that his mother had been a depressed, fragile and easily overwhelmed woman whom he had apparently "transferred" onto me.

This dream was the initial communique about a relationship that was to remain virtually unwavering between us for two and a half years, until a session several weeks before a long summer break, in which the patient began to worry that I had become overwhelmed by my work with him. He explained this in the same way as he had explained the dream, as well as a number of similar episodes that had occurred since his dream, by saying that he knew it was probably a "transference" from past experiences with his mother.

Although I had never really felt satisfied with these interpretations, I also had not been able to see why, and had more or less fallen into the habit of silently assenting to them. But this time I was struck by the lifeless manner with which he spoke, and by the fact that he afterward lapsed into a torpid silence. When he did speak again, I noticed that it was in a cautious and tentative way, being careful (I felt) not to say anything that might cause me any distress or make me feel there was any work I had to do for him. I reflected to myself that, although he had meant by his interpretation that he realized that his state of mind reflected a past reality now dead and inappropriate to the present, he was acting as though I were indeed quite fragile in present reality. His analysis of his state of mind did not seem to meet or affect his actual experience of it; it seemed, rather, to be a half-hearted attempt to talk himself out of his present experience of me by labelling it transference.

I then began to feel an unexpected sense of irritation at the patient's concern about me. If my job was indeed to help him understand what he was experiencing, then his attempt at making my work easier was having the opposite effect: working with such a reticent patient was much harder than with a candid one.

I told him, with some trepidation, that, while he was aware of feeling that I was overwhelmed, and wanted to help me, I thought he was unaware that his reticence was helping to make me helpless. The patient, as I feared, at once felt angry and hurt.[4]

His reaction confirmed a suspicion that was just beginning to dawn on me: despite his interpretation about the past, he still took it as an unquestionable present fact that I was exhausted. From his point of view, his attempts to lighten my burden were then the only possible way that he could hope to help me. My comment could therefore only represent to him my ingratitude for his efforts. Hence his feeling wounded. The unconscious beliefs about my exhaustion on which his reaction rested suggested that he was not just confusing me with a past figure, or having a fantasy (in the ordinary sense of the word) about me in the present, but actually experiencing me in the present as exhausted and overwhelmed by him. I now realized that what had been irritating me was that this experience carried with it a sense of conviction so strong that it seemed to admit literally no doubt. Any interpretation I might make about it was therefore impotent.

He seemed unable, then—despite his evident desire to think about what made him see me as so incapable—to overcome an emotional certainty about my exhausted state that was so fundamental and undoubted that it made serious consideration of any alternative impossible. When I told him this, he again fell silent. But this silence, unlike his previous reticence, had a thoughtful quality to it. When he broke it, he said very soberly that he now realized his analysis had been governed by a profound belief—an unwavering certainty immune to the experience of the analysis—that I was indeed too fragile to bear the burden of him as a patient. He was astonished to find how it had persisted despite the many times he had tried to convince himself it was merely a carry-over from the past. But he now saw, as if for the first time, that it had been both present since the first day and the first dream, and, up until now, completely untouched by interpretation.

I believe that what had happened was that I had managed to convey to him that his "helpful" circumspection and reticence were actually hindering me as an analyst, and turning me into the feckless mother he feared I was. In doing so, I had departed definitively (perhaps for the first time in his 2½ years of analysis with me) from his unshakeable, unconscious belief in my impotence, and thereby established myself as someone separate from what existed in his mind—what we might call a proper object. I had, in other words, broken away from his fantasy and thereby become and object with a mind of its own, separate from his: a whole object.

Over the next few weeks the analysis took on a seriousness and a hopefulness that I had not seen previously. The patient now experienced his listless and oft-repeated formula about his mother not merely as a kind of "analysis" that he didn't really believe in, but as a way of actively wasting his time and life. He felt genuinely guilty (not the false guilt connected to the feeling that he was failing to meet the supposedly unreasonable, infantile demands of his objects), and at the same time began to recognize for the first time the burden he was placing on me, and to appreciate my efforts to help him with himself.

As a consequence of his mourning the waste, his analysis had now come to life, and was not just an exercise in admiring me for producing what he believed on a deeper level be worthless interpretations. He began to experience real love and gratitude for the now rehabilitated analysis. His recognition of me as different from his enduring fantasy about me, along with the recognition of how his fantasy had wasted his analysis, enabled him to see the analysis as something worth loving. This allowed him to begin to contain himself, which is what was manifested as the new seriousness and soberness in his attitude.

Discussion

If we place the paternal model of containment that I have tried to describe, which emphasizes grace under fire, alongside the maternal model of containment, which emphasizes receptivity and sensitivity to the patient's state of mind, we arrive at an understanding of the theory of the container that is richer than what we could arrive at on the basis of either model alone. The maternal model of containment emphasizes receptivity to and contact with the patient's state of mind. This establishes the empathic link needed for analysis. The paternal model emphasizes not being driven to do something as a result of what has been received and contacted. This establishes the analyst as an object distinct from the patient, setting up a kind of barrier between the analyst and the patient that ultimately makes the patient aware of the inevitable gap between herself and the analyst. This in turn ushers in the possibility for the patient to perceive the analyst as a whole object, distinct from the patient's projections, and thus to enter into the depressive position with regard to him.

For containment to occur, the analyst must be in good enough contact with the patient to apprehend intuitively and empathically what the patient is projecting, but must also have a barrier strong enough to withstand the pressure to act —to do something to relieve the situation instead of patiently analysing it—that the projection exerts on him. If the analyst is not driven to act, he has time to think about what the patient has projected. This absorption, distancing and thinking is dream-like and largely unconscious, and is what Bion called reverie. The capacity for reverie on which successful containment depends is a product of both the analyst's contact with the patient and his distance from her. This is the analyst's depressive relationship to the patient.

For self-containment to occur, the patient must be aware of the contact existing with the analyst, but also of the gap separating her from him. Acknowledgment of this gap allows her to see him as a whole object, which is a prerequisite for her feeling the gratitude and love for his containment that is necessary for self-containment to develop. This is the patient's depressive relationship to the analyst.

I have described the maternal model and the paternal as two models of containment. From another perspective, they are a single model of what Klein called the combined parental object—maternal and paternal qualities combined —an internal object that she regarded as the unconscious basis of all creativity. The maternal model alone, without the father, is a pre-Oedipal model of the container, the employment of which makes it difficult to move the patient beyond the pre-Oedipal phase of development, while the combined model I am describing is an Oedipal model that facilitates mature resolution of the Oedipal situation and true maturity.

There is a little-noted passage in *Learning from Experience* in which Bion, discussing the maternal model of containment, says almost in passing that, "If the feeding mother cannot allow reverie or if the reverie is allowed but is not associated with love for the child or its father this fact will be communicated to the infant even though incomprehensible to the infant" (Bion, 1994, p. 36). Reverie seems here to require that the feeding mother love the child's father. What's that got to do with it? And what, if this is a model of psychoanalysis, would the mother's love for the father be modelling? I believe that the father in this model is the Oedipal father—an object that interposes itself between the infant and mother. The mother's love for the father represents an area of her mind that is not centred on the infant. A father must be present in the mother's mind—and so therefore must an Oedipal triangle—if the mother is to properly exercise the reverie her child needs and if her child is to benefit from it. What this is a model of is the analyst's dual allegiance to the patient and to the truth (i.e., realities that impose themselves on her and on her patient). This allegiance to the truth is something in the analyst's work that makes unalloyed devotion to relieving the patient's suffering impossible. In terms of the analytic situation, it prevents the analyst from identifying completely with the patient's suffering, and this makes him—and consequently his patient—aware of the gap between them. The patient must acknowledge, accept and come to love the gap between himself and the analyst—the sense of the analyst's grasp exceeding his own—if he is to achieve true independence and what I am calling self-containment. One implication of this is that the Oedipus complex may not be resolved by identification with the parents. Identification with them, being a defence against awareness of their separateness, is a defence against the pain of the Oedipal situation, which is resolved only by a recognition and acceptance of their separateness.

If we simply equate the theory of the container with the maternal model, we lose sight of the elements in the psychoanalytic situation that require a paternal function. This function defends the analyst's maternal linking and synthesis from the patient's attacks on them. This not only preserves the analysis, but gives the patient an opportunity to recognize her own aggression. It also preserves a gap between patient and analyst, which gives the patient a chance to mourn the analysis and thereby establish, however painfully, the depressive identification needed for real self-containment.

Both of these paternal functions impose painful work on the patient. If we fail to recognize the inevitability of this pain, and fail to recognize paternal containment as an essential function of analysis, we are left with only maternal containment, in the context of which we may be misled into thinking that the patient's pain is a failure of containment, rather than a sign that it may be succeeding.

Notes

1 "No modification" is less revealing than it might appear. I once asked Bion if he ever answered a patient's question—a hot issue in those days of debate about "modifications of analytic technique". He replied that he did whatever he thought might help the analysis. This was typical Bion. What appeared to be an answer to my question was really no answer, but rather a response that helped me focus clearly on my question without answering it.
2 As I indicated above, the theory has since found wide application to a number of problems in psychoanalysis. Since my aim is to identify what is essential in Bion's theory, I will for the time being ignore these later developments, not because they are unimportant, but because they would distract from my main goal.
3 See www.thegazette.co.uk/London/issue/30801/supplement/8439
4 James Strachey (Strachey, 1934) holds that what he called a mutative interpretation is always a crisis for the analyst. I believe that my trepidation was a sign that this interpretation was a mutative one.

Bibliography

Wilfred Bion. *Clinical Seminars and Other Works*. Karnac, London, 1994.

Wilfred R. Bion, *Learning from Experience*. Jason Aronson, Lanham, MD, 1994.

Sigmund Freud. Findings, ideas, problems. *The Standard Edition of the Complete Psychological Works of Sigmund Freud*, 23:299, 1939.

Melanie Klein. A contribution to the psychogenesis of manic-depressive states. In *The Writings of Melanie Klein, Volume 1: Love, Guilt and Reparation and Other Works, 1921–1945*, 262–289. The Hogarth Press, London, 1935 [1975].

Melanie Klein. Mourning and its relation to manic-depressive states. In *The Writings of Melanie Klein, Volume 1: Love, Guilt and Reparation and Other Works, 1921–1945*, 344–369. The Hogarth Press, London, 1940 [1975].

Melanie Klein. The mutual influences in the development of ego and id. In *The Writings of Melanie Klein, Volume 3: Envy and Gratitude and Other Works, 1946–1963*, 57–60. The Hogarth Press, London, 1952 [1975].

John Steiner. *On Seeing and Being Seen*. Routledge, Abingdon, 2011.

James Strachey. The nature of the therapeutic action of psychoanalysis. *The International Journal of Psycho-Analysis*, 50:275, 1934.

11
FINDING THE CONTEXT

Observation

In a paper delivered to the British Psychoanalytical society in 1963,[1] Bion discussed what he called "psychoanalytic statements", defined quite broadly as "anything from an inarticulate grunt to quite elaborate constructions" that somehow communicate an emotional experience. The analyst's first and most important task is to observe these emotional experiences in as much specific detail as he can:

> The more nearly he is able to approximate to this ideal, the nearer he is to the first essential in psycho-analysis ... namely, correct observation. The complement of the first essential is the last essential—correct interpretation. By "first" essential I mean not only priority in time but priority in importance, because if an analyst can observe correctly there is always hope; it is of course a big "if". Without the last essential he is not an analyst, but if he has the first essential he may become one in time; without it he can never become one, and no amount of theoretical knowledge will save him.
> *(Bion, 1997, p. 14)*

Having placed observation of the patient's emotional experiences at the centre of psychoanalytic technique, Bion orients the second part of the analyst's work, determining the meaning of these experiences, around this kind of observation. The major pitfalls in this second part of the work are the analyst's prejudices and pre-conceptions. These troublesome prejudices and pre-conceptions arise from the analyst's hatred of the insecurity and uncertainty attendant on making an observation (that is, emotional contact with something) that is really new and unfamiliar, which drives him to reduce the new observation to something already known, understood and preconceived:

> This brings me to reconsideration of the nature of interpretation ... if observation is sound, the conclusion that certain observed phenomena appear to approximate to a psycho-analytical theory will also be sound. But the soundness of the [observation] is impaired if the theory, which is always a pre-conception ... colours the selection of the facts to be observed ... For if the preconception is psycho-analytical, there is clearly a risk that the observations made under such a pre-conception appear to approximate to a psychoanalytical theory because they in fact derive from it. Such a condition amounts to circular argument.
>
> *(Bion, 1997, p. 14–15)*

He is here reminding us once again that the analyst must not have psychoanalytic theories in mind when he observes the patient, because of the risk that such theories will foreclose observation and lead the analyst to "see" only what he brought to the session.

Clinical illustration

He goes on to illustrate the danger of the analyst's preconception, not by writing about the analyst, but, as he often did, by discussing a patient whose problem is the same as the analyst's, only writ larger. He gives a clinical vignette concerning a patient who,

> though aware of the approach of a car, walked out in front of it, was knocked down, and sustained minor injuries. This result was apparently quite unexpected. Many of his statements had prepared me to expect that he was dominated at the time of the event by the conviction that he was a puff of flatus.
>
> *(Bion, 1997, p. 16)*

He then says that "the statements amounting to an assertion that he was a puff of flatus constitute an example of what I mean by theory" (ibid.).[2] As an analyst, Bion then explores this theory not to determine its empirical validity (which would have been fruitless when dealing with someone dominated by such a belief) but to draw out what it implies—to determine what it means. Asking what one's theory means is clearly different from, and clearly a prerequisite to, determining its empirical validity. (Compare this to W. V. O. Quine's proposal that the unit of empirical significance in a field of investigation is the entire field of investigation—no theory is an island because its meaning depends on a large and indeterminate mass of other theories and ideas to which it is more or less closely connected; Quine 1961.)

Bion considered that the patient walked in front of the car to determine the meaning of his theory, like a psychoanalyst. In psychoanalysis, a feeling is never right or wrong but only meaningful. Any view that the episode was an empirical testing of a hypothesis leads to a dead end. But if it is regarded as a theory first intended to [define something], and thereby to take the first step in establishing the meaning of [what has been defined], certain aspects of the episode become clearer.

(Bion, 1997, p. 16)

But the patient's attempt to determine the meaning of his belief failed because there was nothing in the patient's view of himself—nothing that he could seriously imagine—that differed in any significant way from his theoretical preconception that he was a puff of flatus. Not even being run down by a car could dislodge him from this preconception. Because of this, his view could not be linked to any context other than itself, and therefore no development—no investigation of what his theory meant—was possible.

Bion interpreted that the patient had a fantasy that he was a puff of flatus. But he could not understand this interpretation. Bion gives two reasons for this: the first was his use of the word "fantasy" in his interpretation caused the patient to think of psychic reality, which he was quite loath to do, and the second was that the interpretation as a whole led him to feel that, if the only "evidence" that corresponded to his view of himself (which, we recall, he held as a conviction) was a fantasy, then others would think him mad.

Over the next week or ten days, Bion made many interpretations intended to draw the patient's attention to the rigidity with which he clung to his theory that he was physically insubstantial. "Then, not having directly referred to the episode again after his first mention of it, he said the car driver had called him a fucking fool. I feel better now, he said" (Bion, 1997, pp. 19–20). Bion took this to mean that the patient was now able to entertain a view of himself that differed from his preconceived theory. Bion said to the patient "that he felt the car accident was a sexual intercourse between a puff of flatus and the car and its driver. He said he felt better and added he felt he was going mad."

Bion remarked that, while such a rigid preconception precludes

> the matching or correlation of two statements and is therefore sterile, [it] is preferred [by the patient]. ... because of the risk of a matching of two ideas that is accompanied by a feeling of madness. There is implicit in this the possibility that there must be distance between the correlated statements if meaning is to be achieved. If 'madness' is feared, the operation that leads to meaning is avoided.
>
> *(Bion, 1997, p. 20)*

The driver's view of the patient (that he was "a fucking fool"), when put together with the patient's view of himself (that he was physically insubstantial), spanned a circle of some diameter. What had happened was that the patient had allowed into his mind something outside the compass of his "theory" about himself (namely the driver's view that anyone acting as though he were physically insubstantial while crossing a road must be a fool). This was something to which his theory could be linked, against which it could be compared, and into the context of which it might be set—that is, something that would allow elucidation of the meaning of his preconceived theory. However, it provided little support for the theory to which the patient was committed, a realization that immediately led to another, that his theory might require some modification. The "madness" that he feared was a sense of persecution associated with the ominous feeling that change might be unavoidable. This is a boldface version of the fear that the analyst faces when he makes an observation about a patient that may or may not fit into his preconceived theories (Bion's "first essential" for a psychoanalyst).

When the patient said that the driver of the car had called him "a fucking fool", Bion said that the collision represented an intercourse between a puff of flatus and the car. The fact that the patient could have this association itself meant that the patient could, to however small a degree, entertain the driver's point of view, a view of the patient from a vertex different from that of the patient, alongside his own. This resulted in an intercourse in the patient's mind between his view of himself—that he was a puff of flatus—and the driver's view of him—that he was a fool.

This juxtaposition of two distinct and distant views of the same thing was an enlargement of the circle in which the patient's view of himself travelled. This enlargement corresponds to a psychoanalytic development, which carried with it as by-products the simultaneous feelings that he was better (since he recognized that he was able to allow some other perspective to coexist with his theory of himself, and that he therefore had some potential for development) and that he was going "mad". Here, "mad" refers to his sense that he had a potential for development or change, just as "better" does. The two are experiences of the same thing from rather different points of view.[3]

The patient now could (at least momentarily) entertain a perspective that moved him off the point to which he was fixed and into a broader arc. This was a genuine development. It consisted not of the empirical verification or disconfirmation of the patient's theory, but of a matching of two different views of the same thing that illuminated the structure of his theory and its logic. It did not answer the question, "is this theory true?", but it did give at least a partial answer to the question, "assuming (by definition) that my theory is true in some way, in what way (or context) is it true?"

The answer is "in the context of fantasy only, completely detached from any contact with internal or external reality that might differ from it". This presents the patient with a dilemma. From the point of view of the desire to have one's preconceptions be correct, and moreover the only possible correct ones, anything that differs from the patient's assumption (fantasy) about himself, and which he takes seriously, is madness. From the opposite point of view, the point of view that seeks differing views of the same thing so that the meaning of these views may be gleaned from their juxtaposition with each other (what Bion refers to as "a sexual intercourse"), being stuck in the preconception is madness. So from either perspective, the patient ends up feeling mad. The news that he is mad cannot be very gratifying to the patient, but he also felt better, because knowing he's mad at least helps him to recognize what was trapping him. This provides some relief, however bad the news that occasions it.

Implications

It is quite characteristic of Bion to introduce a discussion of some difficulty facing a practising psychoanalyst by bringing in material from a psychotic patient. It is as though he is saying, "the problems we face when we try to do psychoanalysis are not very different from those of someone who is simply trying to become sane. It is our own tendency toward insanity that presents us with the greatest difficulties in our work."

So he introduces this illustration not simply to give an interesting example of a thought disorder, but also to suggest that when the psychoanalyst is doing psychoanalysis properly, he is doing the same as the patient in his example: he is exploring the meaning (if any) of his own psychoanalytic theories by juxtaposing with them his observations of the patient, which expands the diameter of their admittedly circular argument. An interpretation based only on his theories does not expand them, and does not help the patient. But to the degree that he allows his theories to be brought together with observations that differ from them, the analyst experiences a sense of insecurity (some anxiety in the direction of "going mad"). To come up with a way of looking that does not rest entirely on preconceptions constituted by his theories, the psychoanalyst needs to dislodge himself from his psychoanalytic theories. To the degree that he is successful, he will be able to observe with fresh eyes. This dislodging, however, invites a theoretical vacuum and its accompanying *horror vacui*. The degree to which the analyst may dislodge himself from his preconceptions is limited by this horror, and so therefore is the diameter of the circle he is able to inhabit.

An interpretation contributes to psychoanalytic growth to the degree that it allows one to set one's preconception into context and to learn what was implicit but unrecognized in the terms (i.e. unconscious premises) one began with.

Bion's ideas suggest that an interpretation does no more than illuminate the meaning of our premises; that the patient's theory, the analyst's theories and perhaps all theories, are circular; and that it is the analyst's job to determine what circles they travel in.

We determine the meaning of emotional experiences not by identifying how they fit into our pre-existing theories of the mind, but by locating the context into to which these experiences do fit, regardless of our pre-existing theories: the network of their emotional connections in one's mind. And we illuminate the structure of this network by imagining how the same thing would look from a different view, then juxtaposing the two. This approach constitutes finding the context within which a given point of view is valid.

A working hypothesis

To put it more specifically, psychoanalysis is not interested in the empirical validity of the patient's beliefs—their relationship to external reality—but is instead interested their meaning—their relationship to internal reality. The unconscious premises that make the patient's beliefs make sense are an important part of this internal reality.

It is useful as a working hypothesis to assume that whatever the patient says must make sense, no matter how bizarre it may seem on first acquaintance, and that if it does not appear to do so, it is due to the analyst's failure to understand the context from which the patient is speaking. This "finding the context" is a function of Bion's K, curiosity about the world, and leads to a way of scrutinizing the mind that is the opposite of the "sitting in judgement". It constitutes integrating the patient's ideas into the context of human activity by finding the reason for them, the opposite of condemning them as beyond the pale ("pathological").

Bion was able to accomplish this by sympathetically entering far enough into the patient's world to grasp where he was coming from—what convictions or beliefs underlying the patient's experience must be in force—in other words, by winkling out the context in which the patient's communications and behaviour make sense. Identifying this context makes it possible to put it into words, and to speak of it from the inside and the outside at the same time, as it were. This gives the patient the opportunity to see the same thing simultaneously from the inside (via his own experience) and from the outside, and to develop from the tension between the two. Bion calls this juxtaposition of two different things giving rise to potential new developments an "intercourse" between two points of view. We must take this word seriously, lest we fall into the error of regarding this juxtaposition as a mere metaphysical or logical exercise (like a Hegelian dialectic). While the manifestation of this event may be simply logical or cognitive in the more superficial layers of the mind, in the deeper layer of unconscious psychic reality, it is quite concretely parental intercourse, and the ability to develop psychologically from the experience depends on accepting the reality of these internal parents having intercourse and producing new babies.

Notes

1 "The Grid", published posthumously in *Taming Wild Thoughts* (1997). This is not to be confused with Bion's later paper, also entitled "The Grid", published in 1977.
2 The patient seems to have believed unconsciously that he was insubstantial—pure spirit. The unconscious fantasy underlying this theory was something along the lines of

having created himself out of his own anus as a non-corporeal being; he had idealized his farts and identified himself with them. This may strike some readers as odd, but we have to remember that this is an unconscious fantasy and that the unconscious is another world; they do things differently there.
3   This is an example of what Bion called "binocular vision".

Bibliography

W. R. Bion. *Taming Wild Thoughts*. Karnac, London, 1997.

Willard van Orman Quine. Two dogmas of empiricism. In *From a Logical Point of View*, 20–46. Harper and Row, New York, 1961.

12
SUMMARY AND CONCLUSIONS

From birth and throughout life, we draw on the non-verbal register of song-and-dance as a primordial form of communication. Infants respond to the musical elements of human speech with dance-like movements that keep time with the music. This interaction recruits them into the human linguistic community, and sets the stage for the later acquisition of verbal speech, which is layered over this foundation of non-verbal, musical communication. Not long after birth, this register of communication is joined by a visual track involving the face and eyes: infants need the faces within their field of view to be responsive to them if they are not to fall into a state of isolated despair and inertia.

These discoveries expand our idea of language and communication beyond the verbal realm, and permit a perspective from which verbal communication, far from encompassing all of language, is only a later development that rests on an earlier foundation of music, rhythmic movement and facial expression, acting as a kind of multi-band baby-talk. This expansion of our concept of language echoes the expansion of our concept of mind brought about by the discovery of the unconscious, so that just as we now recognize that the conscious mind, previously thought to be the entire mind, is only its most superficial layer, we now also recognize that the conscious aspects of verbal language are only its most superficial layer.

We may align these two discoveries by postulating that non-verbal modes of communication, operating outside of consciousness, form a direct link between the (non-verbal) unconscious of one mind and that of another, entering conscious life if at all only as a "vibe", a term that reveals its roots in the musical register. Restating this in slightly more rigorous psychoanalytic terms, this mode of communication may form a direct link between one person's unconscious internal world and that of another.

The likelihood of this link is supported by Melanie Klein's discovery of the unconscious internal world, a deep level of the mind in which mental states are experienced in a bodily way. What we experience consciously as our emotions and intuitions are experienced unconsciously as "a multitude of beings which with all their activities, friendly or hostile, lodge[d] inside one's body, particularly in the abdomen" (Melanie Klein Trust papers, quoted in Hinshelwood, 1997, p. 885). Because we experience emotional states in the body, song-and-dance, operating on a sensory level and producing direct physical effects, is a natural mode of communication between one unconscious internal world and another. The internal world is formed, maintained and remodelled in large part by this kind of communication, operating between individuals via the unconscious channel of what Bion called realistic projective identification. Song-and-dance communication links the concrete, unconscious, internal world of one individual to the community of other internal worlds (other unconscious minds) to form social groups in which individuals are bound together by psychological forces far deeper than those of mere social or instrumental advantage.

One type of social group produced by unconscious, song-and-dance communication is characterized by what Bion called basic assumption activity: an automatic and involuntary shared belief in certain ideas supported not by evidence but by their power to produce a sense of security and bondedness. Bion found that that work (contact with reality) produces insecurities that bring into play basic assumption activity as a defence against them. If we imagine a psychoanalysis as a group of two, the work of psychoanalysis consists largely of the study of these basic assumption activities as they operate within this small group. In this view, transference and countertransference are not the past substituted for the present, but the externalization of the internal worlds of the two participants, each making the other an external version of their internal objects. Basic assumption activity—defences against the insecurities that appear in psychoanalytic work—occurs when transferences and countertransference are complimentary. One example of this kind of configuration is the basic assumption activity that we call suggestion.

Psychoanalysis originated in suggestion. When he first began practice, Freud used the power of suggestion to force his patients to recall the traumatic histories that his seduction theory needed them to have. When he discovered transference—one of the two legs on which suggestion stands—he advocated interpreting only those forms of it that led the patient to have negative feelings about the analyst. Transferences that produced positive feelings were to be left uninterpreted, so that they could form the basis of a far more subtle and powerful form of suggestion. The exploitation of positive transference is a manifestation of the analyst's countertransference, which is the other leg on which suggestion stands. Practising suggestion forces the analyst into the position of what Lacan called *le sujet supposé savoir*, someone who is supposed to know the answers in order to provide them to the patient in the form of suggestions. This imperative has driven psychoanalysts into various forms of dogmatism. It remains an open question whether is it possible to overcome dogmatism and avoid suggestion in psychoanalysis.

Suggestion relies on a combination of seduction (playing on the patient's desire to be loved) and intimidation (playing on the patient's fear of being spurned or rejected). In both cases, the analyst is taking advantage of the parental role assigned to him (and the child role assigned to the patient) in the patient's transference. Playing the parental role means that the analyst is passing judgement on how "good" or "bad" the patient is being, as though the patient were a child. Since suggestion rests of a complimentary combination of transference and countertransference, one strategy for avoiding suggestion is for the analyst to escape the grip of his suggestion-friendly countertransference. However, since neither transference not countertransference can be done away with, this strategy fails, and all that the analyst can do is try to recognize his countertransference when it appears, and restrain himself from acting on it in the guise of "therapeutic" activity. Bion has advocated that any desire that the analyst feels for the patient, including, or rather, especially the desire to do something therapeutic, be treated as material for self-analysis.

To the degree that the analyst has been able to work through the countertransferences on which suggestion depends, he will be able to depart from the role of parent—that is, refuse to praise or condemn the patient, however subtly—and to transform the inevitable forces of suggestion (and the transference and countertransference on which they rest) from something interfering with the analysis into the object of its scrutiny. Instead of praising or condemning, the analyst will in the ideal case merely observe how things are, without value judgement or suggestions—either in words, or more importantly, in music—about how they should be.

This is a subtle point. Very few if any analysts will endorse praise or condemnation as good psychoanalytic technique, and all will maintain that they do not practise it. This is true if one restricts oneself to the analyst's conscious, verbal communications to the patient. But if we look at the unconscious, musical register, which is perhaps a more important mode of communication in clinical psychoanalysis than the conscious, verbal register,[1] we see a different picture. In recent years, the International Psychoanalytic Association has sponsored an investigation into how its members work, in which a group of analysts gather to scrutinize in minute detail the work of one member of the group. This has revealed that, although the analyst consciously believes he is implementing one theory of psychoanalytic interpretation and treatment, his actual interpretations often imply quite a different theory. In other words, the analyst may have unconscious theories about the nature psychoanalytic work that have far greater impact than do his conscious theories on how he actually practices.

The analyst's role as a parent in the basic assumption group is intimately linked to the idea of psychoanalysis as a form of treatment along the lines of medical treatment (from which psychoanalysis arose) or the much older tradition of spiritual healing (from which medicine arose). This idea implies that the psychoanalyst must cure something in the patient—either by directly remedying some psychological deficit or by directly providing a correction for some derangement in the patient's mental functioning. Suggestion attempts to do both of these, while psychoanalysis (to the degree that it is free of suggestion) attempts neither. Psychoanalysis, in other words, can escape suggestion only by giving up the idea that it is a cure, leaving in its place only an idea of fostering psychological development. The goal that psychoanalysis pursues in this mode is not cure, but truth (roughly, phenomena whose existence does not depend on the presence of a thinker). Detachment from the goal of cure detaches psychoanalysis from the practice of suggestion, which allows it instead to study suggestion. Making the discovery of truth a prime value places psychoanalysis in a relationship to the transference that is different from that of, say, supportive psychotherapy or behavioural therapy, which "cure" through the practice of suggestion. While supportive psychotherapy and behavioural therapy exploit the transference in the service of suggestion, psychoanalysis explores the transference in the service of establishing the reality of the conscious and unconscious relationships between analyst and patient. Psychoanalysts may use suggestion unintentionally, of course (for instance when the analyst falls into playing a role in the basic assumption group), but, unlike supportive psychotherapy or behavioural psychotherapy, they subject it in the end to study (or try to) once they become aware of it.

In place of offering cure, Bion proposes that psychoanalysis restrict itself to searching for truth. In his view, the search for truth is crucial because, among other things, the only alternative to this search is practising propaganda: the analyst either searches for truth or acts as a propagandist—the enemy of truth and thought. Bion offers a reading of the Oedipus myth as defiance of a god who forbids thought and exploration.[2] Suggestion from this perspective is a form of propaganda, adopted by the analyst as a way of exerting power over the patient's mind, at the expense of the patient's ability to think for himself. Of the three types of links that Bion believed we form with the world, L (love of an object), H (hated of an object), and K (love of truth), only K is free of the desire to control. In fact, the desire to control psychic reality, the goal of suggestion and propaganda, is antithetical to the love of truth (and vice versa). The analyst's capacity to do analysis depends on a radical respect for truth that overcomes his desire to control (of which healing and curing are instances).

How do we study phenomena located in the register of song-and-dance scientifically? Experimental sciences are able to create many precise replicas of the phenomena they study, by virtue of which they are able to create general theories that can substitute for experience. Psychoanalysis can do neither, and seems therefore to be disqualified from scientific status. If, however, we examine how "hard" scientists actually work in day-to-day practice, we find that they are constantly formulating informal, working hypotheses that are temporary, intuitive and disposable (like the scaffolding used in building construction) Psychoanalysis proceeds in much the same way. Much like practitioners of psychoanalysis, practitioners of experimental science use intuition constantly. Psychoanalysis differs from the hard sciences in not having a hierarchical system of theories—

theories subsidiary to fundamental premises. It has only fundamental premises that give rise to an approach or method of studying the mind.

This method is a form of the ancient Greek mode of study called *techne*. It requires open-minded observation based more on assessment of the specific problem at hand than on the use of formal theoretical guidelines, and allows the psychoanalyst to see things beyond his theoretical framework, which is kept in abeyance. He then makes something like an educated guess about the meaning of what he has observed, aided by his receptivity to non-verbal song-and-dance. Official psychoanalysis has attempted to circumvent this character by declaration or fiat asserting that psychoanalysis simply is a science. In contrast, *techne* is a thoughtful examination of the way in which each analysis is carried out. This type of investigation is appropriate to the examination of the mind.

The existence of song-and-dance communication means that suggestion is constantly present in human interactions. Psychoanalysis is the study of spontaneous communication arising in the register of song-and-dance. It provides the patient with a chance to learn about his mode of communication and his mental life, and thereby to play, goallessly, with them in precisely the way that creative scientists play with their data. Projection into the analyst via projective identification/song- and-dance is, among other things, a form of experimentation. The analyst, for his part, reflects on what role the projective identification has cast him into, but does no more. This last is a sign of respect for the patient. The analyst allows the patient to play on him, in order for him to learn about the patient, but does not himself play on the patient.

Bion's theory of the container relies on Klein's "'balance of projection and introjection" but adds a new element—that of detoxification. The maternal model of the container emphasizes understanding and relief. But containment also requires the analyst to stand up to a psychotic part of the patient's personality that tries to destroy the container's ability to contain. Self-containment rests not on identification, as the maternal model implies, but on love for the container in both its gratifying and prohibiting forms—in Klein's terms, a combined parental object—as an object separate from the self. One implication of this is that the Oedipus complex is not resolved by identification with the parents: identification, being a defence against awareness of separateness, is a defence against the Oedipal situation, not a way of acknowledging its reality.

We have been considering both a new register and a new mode in psychoanalysis. The new register is song-and-dance—a musical channel of communication that is primordial, operates in the quasi-physical mode in which unconscious fantasy makes its impact on the mind, and must be intuited rather than reasoned out. The new mode is one in which psychoanalysis breaks free from direct therapeutic ambition and its main tool, suggestion, not by banishing the force of suggestion (which is, of course, not possible in any human activity), but by making it the focus of the investigation, by dispassionately looking, as it were, at the place where passion lives.

In the practice of suggestion, the suggestionist indicates more or less subtly how the patient should think or feel. The power of suggestion rests on the patient's tendency to identify with the suggestionist. In contrast to this, by focussing his interpretations on how the patient is (as opposed to how he or she should be)—that is, by restricting his activity to making the patient conscious of the unconscious context from which his experiences and beliefs arise, the analyst gives the patient an opportunity to identify with himself or herself, not with the suggestionist/therapist, thereby turning the analysis fertile ground for the development of self-containment and psychological development.

In psychoanalysis, empathy is not the analyst's identification with or sympathy for the patient (as it might be if viewed from a moral or "supportive" perspective). It is understanding where patients are coming from solely for the purpose of acquainting them with themselves so they may have minds of their own. No practice other than psychoanalysis has such profound curiosity about individual patients, and no other practice exhibits such profound respect for them.

Notes

1 More important because the patient will listen more to the analyst's tone of voice, word emphasis, and so on, more than the verbal content of interpretations to form an impressions how the analyst "really" feels.
2 This god is similar to the object of worship in Marx's view of religion as an opiate that keeps people from recognizing the reality of their economic situation.

Bibliography

R. D. Hinshelwood. The Elusive Concept of "Internal Objects": Its role in the formation of the Klein Group. *International Journal of Psycho-Analysis*, 78(5): 877–897, 1997.

INDEX

acting out and acting in 78
Adamson, Lauren B. 4
aesthetic conflict 41–43
aesthetic experiences 68–73
anger 82
animism 13
anxieties 31, 40, 81
Aristotle 65
Army, as basic assumption group 15
Army, Bion's experience in 77–78
attacks on linking 79
autism 13n3

baby talk 5
bad objects 76
basic assumption 14–18, 22, 25, 31, 95, 96
behavioural therapy 32, 97
Belle Dame sans Merci 42
Bernheim, Hippolyte 21, 24, 25
bias, analysts' 25
binocular vision 93n3
Bion, Wilfred: analyst's techniques 87–88; on answering patients' questions 85n1; basic assumption mentality 14–15, 16; container/contained 35, 74, 76; curing/healing 34–35, 41, 69; dependency 25; evocation of emotional states in another 9; facts/truth 36–37, 66n2, 97; group work 17; K 37–38, 42; linking 42; maternal model of containment 76–79, 84; military service 77–78; mother-infant relationship 12–13; propaganda 39; psychoanalysis and the search for truth 97; psychoanalytic statements 87; psychoanalytic theory 88–92; realistic projective identification 8, 18; reverie 84–85; on science 45; transference 96; valency 14–15
Bird, Kai 48, 49
bodily sensation, and emotion 11, 95
body language 30, 32, 94–95; *see also* dance
Breuer, Josef 20, 60, 61
British Psychoanalytical society 87

catharsis 21
ceremonial movement 3
chance/uncertainty 65
Charcot, Jean-Martin 56–57
child development: child language acquisition 2, 3, 9–10; favourable environment 79; infant development of the mind 9–10; internal object world 75; and love 12; play 69; unconscious communication 12
Church/religion 15, 44n1, 99n2
combined parental object 84, 98
communication impairments 1
Comparative Clinical Method 29
Condon, William 1, 2, 3, 4, 12, 15
containment 35, 74–87, 98
context, finding the 87–93
counter-suggestion 72
countertransference 17–18, 22, 24–25, 30, 33, 95, 96
creative blocks 61

critical thought 15–16, 31, 37, 68
curing/healing 30–31, 34–35, 69, 96–97

dance 1–2, 3, 9, 11, 94
defense 52, 80, 95
delusion 80
dependency 25
depression 40
depressive positions 84
de-repression 24
detachment 42
detoxification 74, 76–79, 98
discretizing 15, 22
disorganization 4
Dissanayake, Ellen 3
dogmatism 26–27, 95
dream interpretations 61, 81–82
dream-thoughts 13

Eden myth 38
embodied spaces 5, 15, 68, 95
emotional evocation of states in another 9
emotional synchronization 6, 69
emotional turmoil 78
empathy 84, 99
enactment 32–33, 72
envy 40, 41, 80
epistemophilic instinct 42–43
ethical integrity 25
euphoria 3
experience, learning from 39
Experiences in Groups (Bion, 1961) 14
experimental science 45–47, 55–58, 62, 69, 97
externalization of internal world 70, 73, 95

facial expressions 4, 5, 6, 94
fantasy 8, 10, 14, 80, 89, 90
Faulkner, William 22
favourable environment 79
fear 78, 90
feelings 36, 88–89, 95
foetuses' language capabilities 3
free association 40
Freud, Sigmund: epistemophilic instinct 42–43; foetus-infant continuation 7n5; groups 15; identification 80; Oedipus complex 37; projective identification 9; psychoanalytic theory 26, 49; science 55, 56–58; suggestion 19–22, 95; technique 59–64; transference 17, 23–25; unconscious intentions 33n1

Frick, Janet E. 4
fundamental premises 50–53

games 50–53
Garden of Eden 38
Gleick, James 69
good analytic relationships 19
"good patient" mentality 22, 29, 40
grace under fire 78
Groddeck, Georg 73n2
group connection 5
group mentality 14
group movement 3, 4
group solidarity 3, 5, 9
guessing 47, 49, 57, 59–60, 62–63, 98
guilt 40

Hamlet 72
hate 42, 70–71, 80, 97
healing/curing 30–31, 34–35, 69, 96–97
Heisenberg, Werner 53n1
helplessness 71–72, 82
herd animals, humans as 9
hospitalism 13n1
Hume, David 68
hypnosis 19, 60
hypothesis testing 55, 57, 58, 62, 89
hysteria 20–21, 60

identification 79–81, 85, 98; *see also* projective identification
illusion 24
imagination 61
incorporation 79–80
inner worlds, connection with 70, 72–73
insecurity 16, 17, 87, 91, 95
instincts 10; *see also* intuition
interactional synchrony 1
intercourse 89, 90, 91, 92
internal reality 70, 92
internal world: externalization of internal world 70, 73, 95; internal world-external community relationship 10, 95; Klein's internal objects 10, 17, 74–75, 84, 94–95; transference 17; unconscious communication 11
International Journal of Psychoanalysis 27n13
International Psychoanalytic Association 26, 29, 34, 63, 96
interpretations 36, 47, 66, 71, 74, 76, 82, 88, 89
intimidation 29, 32, 96

intonation 2, 3, 4, 29–30
introjection 8, 74–75, 79–80, 98
intuition 10–11, 49–50, 84, 95, 97–98

Johnson, Samuel 44

K 37, 42–43, 45, 97
Klein, Melanie 8, 10, 11, 42–43, 74–75, 79, 80, 84, 94–95, 98
knowledge: desire for 38, 45; K (love of truth) 37, 42–43, 45, 97; and techne 65
Krafft-Ebing, Richard von 21

Lacan, Jacques 25, 79
language genesis 2–3
leadership 15, 25
learning from experience 39
Learning from Experience (Bion, 1962) 12
linking 14, 42, 79, 85, 94–95
love: Bion's L, K and H 42, 97; and containment 81; and identification 80; of mother for father 84; of mother for infant 12; and psychoanalysis 19; and suggestion 24; and transference 23; and truth 37

magic of words 60–61
Maiello, Susan 3
Main, Thomas 72
Malloch, Stephen 4–5, 15, 22, 68
Marx, Karl 44n1, 99n2
materialism 12
maternal model of containment 76–77, 78–79, 80, 83–85, 98
meaningful speech sounds 2
medicine (as discipline) 58–59
Meltzer, Donald 3, 9, 41, 43
Memoir of the Future, A (Bion, 1990) 36
memory 17, 21, 35, 60
mental treatment 58, 59
mind-reading 59, 61
models versus theory 76
mothers: and identification 80; inconstancy 42; infant awareness of mother's voice 3; maternal model of containment 76–77, 78–79, 80, 83–85, 98; reverie 84; transference 82, 83; unconscious communication 12
muscular bonding 3, 4
music: child language acquisition 9, 10; as element of human language 2, 3; and intuition 11; mother-infant communication 5, 9; unconscious communication 11, 15, 29–30, 94, 96, 98

naturalistic observation 56
neuroscience 20
neurosis 78, 79
newborns 1–2, 4–5

objectivity, analysts' 25
observation techniques 57, 69–70, 72–73, 87, 90, 96
Oedipal dilemma 37–44, 51–53, 84–85, 97, 98
omnipotence 8, 15, 18, 34, 81
Oppenheimer, J. Robert 49
O'Shaughnessey, Edna 8–9

panic 78
Pappenheim, Bertha 20
paranoia 42
parent-child relationship 22, 24, 29, 31, 40; *see also* mothers
part-object identification 80
passions 68
paternal model of containment 79–81, 83–85
pathology 32, 42, 58, 76, 92
Paul, Michael 3
personality 26, 63
phantasy 8, 75, 81
philosophy 54, 56, 58, 65, 68
pitch 2
Plato 54
play 68–73
poiesis 62
Poincaré, Henri 66n2
possession 42
praise 29, 96
pre-conceptions 87, 88–91, 92
prejudices 87
projections 70, 74–75, 79, 84, 98
projective identification 8–9, 10, 18, 41, 52, 95, 98
propaganda 37, 39, 41, 97
proto-mental personality 9
psyche 58
psychiatry 31
psychic mediums 59
psychic reality 10, 89, 92, 97
psychoanalysis: Balkanization of psychoanalytic theory 26; craft of 54–67; definitions of 26, 63; Freud's technique 59–64; goals of 30–31; as group activity 17; healing/curing 30–31, 34–35, 69, 96–97; origins of 56–59; psychoanalytic theory 26, 29, 46–50, 51–53, 88; as relationship 69; and

suggestion 19–28; theory of the container 76–77
psychoanalytic statements 87
psychological development 12, 31, 43, 75, 79, 97
psychological pressure 20–21, 22, 60
psychology 31, 52
psychosis 76, 77, 78, 79, 91

Quine, Willard van Orman 88

rapport 6
realistic projective identification 8, 18, 95
reason 61, 68
receptors for love 12
relief, psychoanalysis providing 77
replicability, scientific 46
representational fidelity 61
repression 17, 20, 21, 22, 24, 39, 59, 60
re-repression 59
resistance 3, 21, 30, 55, 59, 60
reverie 76, 79, 84–85
rhythm 1, 2, 3, 6, 9–10, 30, 94
Rickman, John 53n2
riddance 42
Romanticism 58–59
rules 50–53

Sander, Louis W. 1, 2
sanity/madness 89–91
scaffolding 48–49
scepticism 16
Schiller, Friedrich 61
schizophrenia 34, 41
Schlossman, F. E. 13n1
science: and children 69; defiance of taboos 44n3; empirical investigations 88; experimental science 45–47, 55–58, 62, 69, 97; hypothesis testing 55, 57, 58, 62, 89; and psychoanalysis 26, 34, 45–53, 54–56, 58–59, 62–63, 97–98; replicability, scientific 46
security 38–39, 95
seduction 20–21, 29, 32, 72, 95, 96
self-analysis 96
self-containment 74, 79–81, 84, 85, 98, 99
self-hatred 70
self-knowledge 37
self-multilation 42
self-object relationships 80–81, 83, 84
self-synchrony 1
semantics 2, 5, 11
sense of belonging 15
sensory apparatus 11, 95

separation 5, 42, 81, 84, 85, 98
sexual abuse 20, 21
sexual excitation 20, 21
sexual pleasure 38
Shakespeare, William 72
shared organization 2, 4, 5, 12, 15, 19
Sherwin, Martin J. 48, 49
silence 82, 83
solidarity 3, 5, 9
Spilius, Elizabeth 8–9
spiritual healing 96
splitting 39
Steiner, John 81
still-face experiment 4, 15, 69
Strachey, James 74, 85n4
suggestion: basic assumption mentality 18n2; Oedipal dilemma 39; and play 68, 69, 72; and psychoanalysis 19–28, 29–33, 95–96, 97, 98–99
supportive psychotherapy 32, 97, 99
symbolism 10, 11
synchrony 1, 2, 5, 6, 15, 68

taboos 44n3
tacit agreements 19
Tavistock Institute 14, 17
techne 56, 62, 64–66, 98
thought disorders 76
timing 30, 32
tone of voice 29–30, 32, 99n1
transference: analyst as parent 82, 96; containment 83; Freud, Sigmund 95; psychoanalysis explores not exploits 97; suggestion 22–25, 27, 29, 30, 32, 95; unconscious communication 17–18; *see also* countertransference
trauma 20–21, 95
treatment 30–31, 96
Trevarthen, Colwyn 4–5, 15, 22, 68
Tronick, Edward 4, 69
tropisms 14, 15
truth: and Bion's "K" 43; and containment 85; and the goals of psychoanalysis 43, 97; and the Oedipal dilemma 37–39; and psychoanalysis 24–25, 31, 35–37; and science 48

unconscious: analyst's unconscious intent 30, 37, 96; as basic premise of psychoanalysis 51, 52, 55–56, 59; and the body 10; connections 6; and creativity 84; enactment 32–33; fantasy 92n2; Freud 9; intercourse 92; internal world 11, 75, 94–95; neurosis 79; realistic projective

identification 95; and suggestion 25; as unseen force 56, 69
unconscious communication: analyst-patient relationship 96; beyond suggestion 29–30; dynamics of 14–18; Freud's technique 59–60; intuition 10–11; psychoanalysis as relationship 69; song-and-dance 1–7, 9, 94
unconscious needs 31

valency 14–15
Vassalli, Giovanni 27n13, 54–67
Vienna Medical Society 21

Weinberg, Joe 48, 49
Williams, Meg Harris 42, 43
wish-fulfillment 62
Wittgenstein, Ludwig 50, 54
work group activity 16–17